W9-DIE-413

The NEW
Administrative Professional

From Administrative Assistant
To Administrative Professional

by

Paul A. Douglas, Ph.D.

BELFAST BOOKS

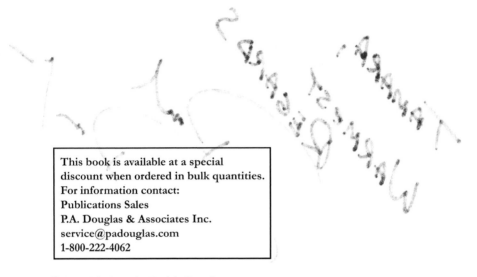

This book is available at a special
discount when ordered in bulk quantities.
For information contact:
Publications Sales
P.A. Douglas & Associates Inc.
service@padouglas.com
1-800-222-4062

Library of Congress Control Number: 2010906709

Library and Archives Canada Cataloguing in Publication

Douglas, Paul A. (Paul Alan), 1947-

    The NEW Administrative Professional / by Paul A. Douglas - 2nd Ed
    p. cm.
    Includes bibliographic references and index
    ISBN 978-0-919917-09-5
    1. Emotional Intelligence 2. Organizational behavior 3. Managing your boss
4. Administrative assistants I. Title

BF576.D69 2010   152.4   C2010-903503-8

This publication is produced to provide current authoritative information on the subject
matter covered. It is sold with the express understanding that the author and/or publisher is
not engaging in rendering psychological, legal, or other professional services. If legal,
psychological, or other expert assistance is required, a competent professional should be
sought.

Printing number
10 9 8 7 6 5 4 3

To My Father

Thomas Douglas. By your example, you taught me what true emotional intelligence is.

Contents

Preface

For the last 38 years, I've had the good fortune and distinct privilege of working with almost 100,000 administrative professionals from virtually every major public and private organization in North America. I've been witness to enormous changes that have taken place in terms of both the responsibilities and duties of administrative professionals, as well as the perceived importance of their role to the organizations they serve.

I have seen job titles change from secretary to executive secretary to administrative assistant to administrative professional.

From this perspective, it's clear to me that a paradigm shift has taken place with regard to the position of the administrative professional in society. Not only has the role of the administrative professional changed, but also the way in which we look at the role has changed.

Many of the responsibilities that were clearly the perquisite of middle managers through the last few decades of the twentieth century are now being handed off to, and being handled by, administrative professionals.

Technical innovation in the workplace, as well as societal changes, not the least of which being never-ending financial constraints with their drumbeat of "do more with less," have seen organizational re-engineering that has greatly influenced the role of administrative professionals.

There is a lag however between the educational needs of this important group and the training and preparation provided to it. To a great degree, much of the training (a word that itself is problematic) provided to those destined to become administrative professionals remains aligned with the needs of yesterday.

Purely technical skills, such as typing or dictation, have been almost altogether supplanted by the need for good organizational and communication skills. As well, increasingly more and more administrative professionals are being asked to supervise the work of other team members.

This book attempts to fill in some of the gaps by providing practical skills and knowledge relevant to the needs of today's administrative professional.

It is my hope that this book may help you better prepare and respond to the challenges and changes that will clearly take place in the next decade.

Paul A. Douglas
March 30, 2011

Chapter 1

The New Middle Management:

The Changing Role of the Administrative Professional

A number of societal and organizational factors have come together to impact the role of administrative professional.

Unquestionably, the evolution from secretary to administrative assistant to administrative professional has been facilitated more than anything by changes that have taken place in the role of middle management in organizations over the past several decades. Administrative professionals are now handling many of the responsibilities that once were the perquisite of middle management.

An appreciation of why this paradigm shift has occurred is basic to our understanding of the current role of the administrative professional, as well as a best guess as to what the future may hold.

In the beginning there was the word, and the word was "control."

As the power and influence of the king or chief or founder expanded, he was no longer able to individually control and oversee every aspect of his realm, organization, or business. It became necessary, therefore, to hire agents to ensure that his interests were being cared for. "Command and control" was the order of the day.

In this world, workers had generally poor qualifications, no autonomy, and trust was not a common value. Simply stated, in the beginning, the primary and essential role of these agents of the leader, was to stand behind workers and prod them to action. These agents or, "middle men," represented the leader's power to sanction in the field.

When seeking to control the labor of a shiftless, poorly qualified, and dependent workforce however, the span of that control; that is, the ratio of managers to workers needed to be relatively small. This meant that more managers were needed to manage the managers, and so on and so on.

Purely in terms of governance, particularly when labor was cheap and readily available, this model worked well; however, the bloated bureaucracies that resulted slowed a company's reaction time. As well, the very nature of these bureaucracies caused decisions to be made far from those most knowledgeable about the situation on the ground and were often based on incomplete information.

The twentieth century produced mega corporations built on large-scale mass production of affordable goods and services. Organizing ways to accomplish this work became an arduous task. Layers of middle management were created to oversee legions of workers and supervisors.

Through the years of rapid growth following the Second World War, middle management continued to grow even more rapidly, outpacing every other organizational component. The organization man, "the man in the gray flannel suit," became the model of middle-class success and normalcy.

As society evolved, however, the role of middle management evolved with it. The carrot-and-stick philosophy was replaced with participatory management, with its focus on the qualitative or human side of management, and this new mantle was placed squarely on the head of the middle manager.

Massacre in the Middle

In the late 1970's and continuing through the 1980's, things began to change more dramatically. A meltdown was evidenced in every sector of the economy. News of layoffs and cutbacks appeared almost on a daily basis. "AT&T cuts 40,000 jobs, 11,500 from middle-management ranks. Union Carbide tags 4,000 middle-management jobs for elimination. General Motors slashes 25,000 jobs and seeks ways to eliminate another 15,000, Exxon reduces its headquarters staff from 2,300 to 325." The same cutbacks were taking place in thousands of less visible companies all across America.

This sudden drive to "thin" the ranks of middle management resulted in a transferring of managerial responsibilities elsewhere within the organization. It created a vacuum that drew many secretaries and administrative assistants unknowingly, if not through the glass ceiling, up against it. More and more administrative professionals, as we refer to them today, were involved in activities that were once the sole perquisite of middle management.

This structural change was witnessed by the fact that the number of administrative support positions in the United States increased from 7.63 to 17.56 million positions (or 130%) during that period, while middle management positions decreased just as dramatically.

The Ubiquitous PC

A second major driving force, which ran concurrently with and contributed to, the downsizing and re-engineering of middle management, was the introduction and almost universal acceptance of the personal computer.

These ubiquitous machines were now performing many of the activities that once kept scores of office workers busy. Fewer workers meant fewer supervisors, which meant fewer managers.

Perhaps even more significantly, the advent and pervasiveness of the personal computer moved many word-processing and later electronic communication responsibilities directly to the manager's desk, many managers, and even executives, began creating at least some of their own documents and communicating electronically.

Emails began replacing letter writing as they were better suited to business communication, short, simply addressing the points involved without rambling. Managers and administrative professionals alike recognized that emails sped things up, making business run more efficiently, no more waiting several days for an airmail letter containing important contracts to arrive when it could be shot to the other side of the world in mere seconds.

Because of this timesaving and the fact that managers were doing more of their own written communication, the administrative professional had more time to take on other responsibilities. These were often the responsibilities that once belonged to the middle manager.

Were it not for this concurrent technological innovation, it would have been unlikely that the administrative professional would have filled the gap created by reductions in the ranks of middle management, at least not as rapidly and pervasively as they did.

The "Second Wave" of the Women's Movement

Clearly, the "second wave" of the women's movement arising in the 1980s had an impact on every level of society and was a key contributor to change.

While the "first wave" of the feminist movement focused largely on overturning legal obstacles to equality, such as voting and property rights, the "second-wave" of the women's movement addressed a wide range of issues and de facto inequalities in the area of sexuality, family, reproductive rights, and issues relating to the workplace.

While it is true that American society was colored increasingly by a conservative political climate in the 1980s, feminists pressed on, maintaining pressure on legislators to address women's issues such as reproductive rights, pay equity, affirmative action, and sexual harassment.

The rights that women fought for, clearly helped working women in a very real way, and organizations that did not respond in an inclusive way to this important change suffered significant internal and external pressures and sanctions.

The Civil Rights Movement

Running concurrently with the women's movement was the civil rights movement, which was initially greeted with as much enthusiasm as the women's movement by the power elite. Organizations not only had to be sensitive to the rights and opportunities they afforded visible minorities but were also under considerable pressure to ensure that their racial mix approximated the general population.

The Embrace of the Team Concept

I believe that the emergence of, and interest in, the team organizational model also dramatically changed the face of American business and industry.

There are four reasons why, beginning in the late 1970s and through the '80s and '90s, team structures became more prevalent.

Looking at the accomplishments of their global competitors, American management attributed much of their success in part, to their team-oriented management style. Japan and Sweden in particular, two countries steeped in the team form of organization, were used as the poster children of organizational peace and profitability.

North America was dragged kicking and screaming into a world of global competition. In the automobile industry, for example, we learned quickly that there were some pretty savvy competitors in Asia. We learned that these competitors could build cheaper cars, better cars, and safer cars than we could. More and more quality offshore products were being imported into the United States. Initially American management pointed to the lower labor rates in some of these countries, it soon became evident that these quality goods were brought to market by motivated, hard-working workers managed effectively through team structures. Structures in which people mattered.

Secondly, American academics and management consultants were able and anxious to present a great body of knowledge and research showing that teams tended to be more creative, responsive, effective, and, perhaps most importantly, cost-efficient than hierarchical organizational structures.

As well, quality-of-work-life studies indicated that participants in ongoing, cohesive teams, given wide latitude in self-management, tended to be more responsible, more highly motivated, and produced superior work.

The third reason why there was a movement towards teams in this period was that we were moving, at that time, into the information age.

When I took my M.B.A. back in the 1970s, I remember reading a book by Harvard sociologist Daniel Bell, entitled "The Coming Post-Industrial Society[3]" in which Bell suggested that in the brave new world of the future, information would replace capital as the prime mover in our economy. Well, by the 1980s, we were there. Information-age companies such as Microsoft, Intel, and Disney were replacing the economic growth engines of the past such as railways, steel manufacturers, etc.

Obviously, in the information economy, greater flexibility and a more rapid response to a changing environment were essential. Team structures provided for the quick reactions necessary.

Fourth, because of the sizable reduction in the ranks of middle management's span of control, the ratio of supervisors to workers, increased significantly. Rather than one manager overseeing the work of eight or nine workers, it was now quite common to see one supervisor for fifteen to twenty employees. When you have the work of up to twenty people being managed by one person, new models and approaches attract greater interest.

Managing the "human resource," as it became commonly known became the subject of considerable interest, research and analysis.

Cultural Shift

Finally, the reason why I believe we have moved and will continue to move towards the embrace of team structures is that we have encountered a cultural shift. Young people coming out of high school, let alone college, expect to be empowered from day one. Perhaps it's the influence of the media, but young people today have no stomach for paying their dues, the way most people of my generation and perhaps yours did. Team structures provide a greater sense of empowerment by allowing even lower-level participants in the organization meaningful levels of involvement and decision-making.

So this brings us to where we are today, a politically correct world where interpersonal sensitivity and the quality of our social dialogue are essential to our overall success.

Chapter 2

Skills for the Information Age

The new reality demands new skills.

Clearly, the administrative professional has moved from specialist to generalist.

The secretary was a specialist. He or she had well defined duties – dictation, typing, filing, etc. Technical skills were not just important; they were paramount.

Traditionally, the secretary supported the manager or executive by helping to manage schedules, control visitors and telephone calls and produce letters and other documents.

The secretary's success did not come from expanding his or her role or even increasing responsibilities, but rather from increasing competence in technical skills. Words per minute in typewriting, and dictation speed in shorthand, were largely the measure of the secretary's worth.

Today most administrative professionals continue to perform many of these traditional roles but clearly to a lesser degree, and unquestionably, to be identified as an outstanding administrative professional, much more than superior technical skills are needed.

As we had mentioned in the last chapter, today many managers handle much of their own correspondence with the help of their own computers storing their files electronically.

Many administrative professionals have moved into training, supervision, research, information management, and many other realms of responsibility. They are involved in project management, equipment evaluation and purchase, as well as customer and public relations.

If it is true that administrative professionals are the new middle management, then it follows that the skills of management and supervision are essential to the assumption of that role.

Inventory of Administrative Professional Competencies

Each year, for the past two decades, I have asked participants at my public administrative professional seminars to complete the Inventory of Administrative Professional Competencies Questionnaire.

Specifically, from a list of 20 skill or competency areas, participants were asked to indicate how much time (hours per week) they were spending utilizing a skill.

This research produced some interesting results, both in terms of the relative value of each competency but also in terms of the comparative significance of emergent skills.

As well, certain trends were observed.

Firstly, the results indicated two clear sets of skills accounting for almost all of the administrative professional's time at work.

These two broad divisions or skill sets may be referred to as Strategic Skills and People Skills.

Strategic Skills

- o Planning, Organizing, and Time-Management Skills (This category also included organizing the manager's schedule, making travel arrangements, etc.)

- o Use of Memory Skills (This included preparation for speeches, presentations; remembering verbal instructions, names, and faces.)

- o Written Communication Skills

- o Meeting-Planning Skills, Minute-Taking, Facilitation, etc.

- o Project Management Skills

- o Computer and Software Skills

People Skills

- o Interpersonal and Communication Skills

- o Team-Building Skills (Including Manager/AP Partnering)

- o Presentation and Public-Speaking Skills

- o Leadership and Supervision Skills

- o Dealing with Difficult People

- o Stress and Conflict-Management Skills

Our research has shown that over the last two decades, administrative professionals spent more than 93% of their time in the above areas of competency.

Looking at the last ten years alone, in terms of the greatest decrease in time allotted, the two biggest losers were:

1. Written Communications (- 28%)
2. Minute Taking, Meeting Facilitation (- 24%)

The biggest increases were seen in the following three areas:

1. Interpersonal and Communication (+ 23%)
2. Leadership and Supervision (+19%)
3. Team Building and Partnering with Manager (+ 17%)

Overall, administrative professionals were spending less time on strategic skills and more of their time on people skills, although some of the strategic skill areas also trended up (problem-solving and presentation skills).

Threshold Skills

Increasingly, technical skills are becoming almost threshold skills – skills required to get the job but not to truly succeed in it.

It was clear from our research that the administrative professional requires skills in management functions and technology, including project management, integrated computer software applications, as well as management-level presentation skills.

Our research confirmed that administrative professionals were handling a wide variety of duties reflecting their increased responsibilities. Today's admin pros are often involved in the purchase of office equipment, the planning of special events, the creation and delivery of presentations, as well as the interviewing and supervision of other staff.

The work we did in this area seems to correlate with the research done by the International Association of Administrative Professionals (IAAP)[2] which recently suggested that a true administrative professional should, in addition to the traditional skills, possess the following competencies and qualities:

- Skill in new and emerging technologies - computer software applications, Internet communications, and research.

- Ability to act autonomously, making decisions independently.

- Possess broad skills in such areas as accounting, interviewing, hiring, and training.

- Demonstrate strong interpersonal skills, including effective listening, strong negotiating, and oral communication skills.

- Be flexible. Have the ability to shift gears effectively and "go with the flow" if things get hectic.

- Be results-oriented. Have the ability to meet deadlines and set and achieve personal goals.

- Have the ability to take initiative.

- Possess an innovative spirit, searching for new, more efficient ways of doing things.

- Have the ability to set priorities with little guidance.

- Have the ability to multitask.

- Be able to participate in group discussions, meetings, and work teams - not just as a scribe.

- Be able to remain unstressed in the face of chaos!

Unquestionably, the advent of the information age and the flattening of our organizational structures have impacted the role of administrative professionals as it has few others.

Clearly, the hard skills (or what we have referred to as "strategic skills") are no longer paramount. It is the "soft skills," or people skills, that have increasingly become essential to the organizational success of the administrative professional.

It is important that, as an administrative professional, you honestly assess your strengths and weaknesses in this area, because the more of these essential soft skills an employer sees in you and reads about in your résumé, the better your chances of recognition and advancement.

When employers are asked what it is they look for in an administrative professional, their common responses are:

Communication Skills

Often the first qualification listed by employers today is, "communications skills." Organizations today are looking for administrative professionals who can listen attentively, speak precisely, and write well. Employers recognize that without clear communication, no aspect of an organization will work effectively; not sales, not production, not management, and certainly not customer service.

Flexibility & Insight

There is a lot more managing going on in companies, both large and small, than can be handled by people with "manager" in their titles. Administrative professionals are now responsible for coordinating multiple tasks, adjusting to an ever-changing environment, setting priorities, directing team efforts, and "managing" their bosses. What employers are looking for are administrative professionals who can quickly assess a situation, figure out what to do and when to do it, without undue stress.

Interpersonal Skills & Leadership

The way in which the administrative professional can relate to people and resolve conflicts – and, if a senior administrative professional or supervisor, motivate and lead others, is critical today. Organizations benefit from having "relationship-builders" who can help achieve consensus and deal with difficult people in a firm but responsive manner.

The administrative professional's ability to motivate, mobilize, and mentor others in the pursuit and attainment of high-performance standards is a true measure of their leadership ability.

Although of late some improvements have been made, educational institutions generally have been slow to respond to the expanded role of the administrative professional.

When you examine the curriculum of many community and business colleges, you find that the majority of their training is focused on the development of technical skills. It would seem that they assume that their students are "up to the job" in terms of their people skills or that they can develop those skills on the job.

When it comes to the training and education of administrative professionals, there is clearly a gap between what is being taught and what is really needed to succeed in that role.

Many companies like my own have emerged to help bridge this gap and assist administrative professionals embrace the new reality by offering management and interpersonal skills training seminars. But for many administrative professionals not afforded these opportunities, it is a matter of picking up the required skills on the job.

This book was written to help administrative professionals by providing the emotional intelligence skills and practical advice that one would find at our high-end workshops.

The focus is on the development of those skills and that specialized knowledge that major public and private organizations, as well as administrative professionals themselves, have indicated are the most critical, relevant, and needed.

Chapter 3

Emotional Intelligence

Clearly, organizations have changed and our role within them has changed and will continue to change.

Success today is not solely determined by how smart you are or how much education you have, or even how well you can do the job from a purely technical perspective. Research conducted throughout the eighties and the nineties and now on the cusp of the new millennium has consistently shown that when people fail at work, they do so largely for one reason, they are unable to work effectively with other people. And whether you are a CEO, or a middle manager, an engineer or an administrative profession, a lawyer or a janitor, your success depends on your ability to work well with others. Regardless of your technical skills, if you don't have that skill you will not reach your full potential.

This new measure of success is being used increasingly in recruitment, promotion, and even termination.

It's not always the most intelligent people who obtain the greatest success. It is not always the hardest-working manager or executive that gets the brass ring. We see examples of this everywhere, in our schools and churches; we see it in politics and the world of entertainment; and we certainly see it in our organizations.

We witness talented, dedicated, hard-working individuals struggling, while those with fewer skills, abilities, and technical know-how thrive and seem to coast to success, and we ask ourselves why this is the case. The answer almost certainly relates to their ability to get things done with and through other people, to influence others in positive ways. Those who consistently come out on top possess what we might refer to as "emotional intelligence."

Emotional intelligence (EQ) is one of the most interesting and worthwhile concepts to hit the business world in recent years. It is based on the notion that the ability of individuals to understand their own emotions, and those of the people they work with, is the key to better interpersonal and organizational success.

Emotional Intelligence Defined

But what is emotional intelligence?

Attempts to define it are difficult because it seems somewhat intangible. It is certainly something that's more difficult to identify on a résumé than education or job experience, but its relevance and importance cannot be overstated.

The best definition I have seen comes from a paper by John D. Mayer of the University of New Hampshire and Peter Salovey of Harvard[4]:

"Emotional intelligence refers to an ability to recognize the meanings of emotion and their relationships, and to reason and problem-solve on the basis of them. Emotional intelligence is involved in the capacity to perceive emotions, assimilate emotion-related feelings, understand the information of those emotions, and manage them."

Emotional intelligence has proven to be an effective tool in human resource development because the EQ principles provide a new way to understand and assess people's behaviors, attitudes, interpersonal skills, and potential.

It can also be an important consideration in human resources planning, recruitment interviewing, as well as management development, customer relations, and more.

The emotional intelligence construct is a relatively new behavioral model. Psychologists Howard Gardner[5] of Harvard, Peter Salovey[6] of Yale, as well as John D. Mayer[7], David R. Caruso[8], and others, did the seminal work on the theory during the 1970s and 1980s. The model and the term "EQ," however, only rose to prominence in 1995 with the publication of Daniel Goleman's[9] book entitled "Emotional Intelligence."

Beyond IQ

The impetus for research on emotional intelligence can be traced back to the 1920s.

At that time a great deal of research was being done to try to determine and measure differences in cognitive ability and intelligence. The thrust came from industry and its desire to predict, from amongst many applicants for a position, who would most likely succeed in that position and demonstrate high levels of performance.

The intelligence quotient (IQ) test that came out of this initial work, again done at Princeton University, provided an objective measure of intelligence. The IQ test was certainly successful in measuring cognitive abilities, logical reasoning, spatial skills, understanding analogies, etc., independent of learning and education. In other words, the test was designed in such a way so as not to be influenced by a person's education or what they had already learned. The test was designed to measure innate mental capacity, the ability to learn.

Industry, however, was disappointed with the IQ test insofar as it was effective in determining who had the highest IQ, and it was far less successful in predicting who the highest job performers would be. IQ was very good at predicting academic potential.

There was a very low correlation between a high score on the IQ test and organizational, financial, or relationship success.

Many people with fabulous IQ scores do poorly in life, wasting away their potential by behaving and communicating in ways that obstruct their chances of success and happiness.

Perhaps you have known someone who, although academically brilliant with superior intelligence, was socially inept.

Although I've long ago stopped going to my high school and university reunions, I went to enough to notice that it was not always the smartest student in high school or college that was the most successful person in the room; in fact, it was rarely the case, especially if we're measuring success by financial and career achievement.

Williams Spady[10] and others have done some interesting research in tracing the lives and careers of valedictorians. The valedictorian, of course, in high school or college is, in almost all cases, the most academically accomplished student, the student with the highest GPA.

Spady[9] found that the career status of valedictorians was subpar, even dismal. He found that large numbers were unemployed or underemployed. It seemed that they were unprepared for the fast-changing post-industrial economy that lay beyond the walls of the university.

In another 14-year study on achievement, Karen Arnold[11] found that at all levels of education; it was hard work and the ability to work with others, as opposed to natural ability or intelligence, which correlated highest with success.

The powerful research conducted at Yale University in the 1980s began by asking the question, "If it's not intelligence that correlates the highest with career success and happiness, what are the factors that contribute?"

What they found was quite surprising but also encouraging. They found that certain qualities, independent of intelligence and relating more to one's ability to work well with other people, correlated highly with career and organizational success and happiness in life generally.

The reason I say "encouraging" is because they also found that unlike IQ, which is basically unchangeable (your IQ will be the same at 16 as 60), emotional intelligence was a very flexible skill that could be changed.

The Building Blocks of Emotional Intelligence

Your emotional intelligence is derived from four elements that are strongly interrelated. These four components are further divided into two primary competencies: personal competence and social competence.

Personal Competencies

Self-Awareness

Self-awareness is the ability to accurately perceive the emotions you are feeling as you are feeling them, and understand why you are having them and what effect they might have. It is the ability to understand the connection between what you are feeling and how you typically respond to those feelings. In other words, it is recognizing the link that exists between your feelings and what you think, do, and say.

Self-awareness also involves a degree of self-honesty, as it implies an awareness of your strengths and weaknesses and is intertwined with confidence and self-esteem, Daniel Goleman[8], in many ways the father of the emotional intelligence movement, says that of all the competences, self-awareness (knowing one's internal states, preferences, resources, and intuitions) is the key to increased personal and organizational performance.

What distinguishes great leaders from those who are just average is their level of emotional intelligence, according to Goleman[8]. From research carried out in the 90s, he found that emotional intelligence proved twice as important as IQ and technical skills. Self-awareness is the core emotional intelligence skill upon which all other emotional intelligence skills depend. Without self-awareness, leadership becomes just another exercise in ego gratification. Self-awareness allows for self-discipline and self-control.

Self-Management

Self-management speaks to your ability to keep disruptive emotions and impulses in check. People with high self-management skills can stay composed and positive under pressure and stress.

Those with good self-management skills exhibit high standards of honesty and integrity; they act ethically and build trust through their reliability and authenticity. They take responsibility for their personal performance and are willing to admit their own mistakes and shortcomings.

Another feature of self-management is flexibility in handling change. People with this competence are innovative; they are comfortable with and open to new and novel ideas. People with high self-management skills are results-oriented and self-motivated. They display optimism and are persistent in pursuing goals despite obstacles and setbacks.

In short, self-management is the ability to keep troublesome emotions and impulses in check, preserve high standards of honesty and integrity, take responsibility for their own performance, and handle change effectively.

Social Competencies

Social Awareness

Social awareness is the ability to sense, comprehend, and react to others' emotions. Individuals with high social awareness are attentive to emotional cues and listen well. They show sensitivity in trying to understand others people's perspectives.

People with this competency focus on the needs of others and are typically good delegators. They acknowledge and reward other people's strengths and accomplishments. They offer practical feedback identifying areas in which improvement is needed.

People with this competency understand customer and client needs and are service-oriented.

They can lever diversity and possess a natural respect for people from divergent and varying backgrounds and are sensitive to group differences. They demonstrate a keen political awareness and can read key power relationships. Above all, they are empathetic, sensing others' feelings and taking an active interest in their concerns.

Relationship Management

The second component of social competence is relationship management. Your skill and adeptness in managing your relationships is dependent, however, on your skill level in the other three components of emotional intelligence.

Relationship management is a measure of your proficiency in managing relationships and building social networks and most important, influencing the behavior of others to positive outcomes. It is the ability to find common ground and build trust and rapport. The following are key indicators of this vital emotional intelligence skill:

- Effectiveness in managing change
- Skill-influencing and persuading
- Capacity to team-build
- Ability to communicate effectively

Relationship management speaks to your ability to use your understanding of emotions (your own and other people's) to manage interpersonal relationships successfully. Relationship management is the essential component of leadership. Relationship management is the ability to inspire others and to arouse enthusiasm for a shared vision.

People who possess high relationship-management skills are able to manage conflict well, while being able to resolve disagreements through negotiation and compromise. They handle difficult people with tact and diplomacy and can focus on the task while at the same time paying attention to relationships. Champions and catalysts for change; they recognize the need for it and work to remove barriers to its fulfillment.

Chapter 4

Emotional Intelligence Inventory

Instructions:

The Emotional Intelligence Inventory (EQI) consists of 40 bipolar statements. Please read both statements carefully, then circle the number CLOSEST to the statement that describes your behavior or belief more. For example, if you feel the statement on the right describes your behavior or belief more than the statement on the left, you would circle the "2." If, on the other hand, you find that the statement on the left best describes your behavior or belief, you would circle number "0." Circle the "1" if you feel both statements reflect your personality or belief equally, you disagree equally with both statements or you simply cannot make up your mind. Please circle just one number per item and answer every question.

Emotional Intelligence Inventory©

Agree with the statement on the left ———

Agree with both
statements equally

——— Agree with the statement on the right

	0	1	2	
1. I am not really in touch with my emotional state.	0	1	2	1. I am keenly aware of my emotional state.
2. I am not really aware of my strengths and limitations.	0	1	2	2. I am fully aware of my strengths and my limitations.
3. I can't say I am really aware of how my behavior affects others.	0	1	2	3. I am fully aware of how my behavior affects other people's feelings.
4. My emotions do not sway my judgement.	0	1	2	4. I know my feelings sway my judgement.
5. I know my self-esteem is lacking. I do not always feel good about who I am.	0	1	2	5. I have great self-esteem and I am totally comfortable in my own skin.
6. Even when I do my best, I feel guilty about the things I did not do perfectly.	0	1	2	6. I am a competent and capable person. I do my best and move on.
7. I often feel bad for no reason.	0	1	2	7. When I feel bad, I always know what's bothering me.
8. I do not sense and understand my emotions as they are happening.	0	1	2	8. I sense and understand my emotions as they are happening.
9. I find it hard to realize how the actions of others affect my emotional state.	0	1	2	9. I realize how the actions of others affect my emotional state.
10. I am not really in touch with my emotions - what they are or why I am feeling them.	0	1	2	10. I am in touch with my emotions - what they are and why I am feeling them.

Emotional Intelligence Inventory©

	Agree with both statements equally		

Agree with the statement on the left ——

—— Agree with the statement on the right

Left statement	0	1	2	Right statement
11. Not all change is good. I approach change very cautiously.	0	1	2	11. I am adaptive and embrace change quickly.
12. I sometimes let people down, not following through on my promises.	0	1	2	12. My word is my bond. People can count on me.
13. I lose my temper too often.	0	1	2	13. I maintain great self-control and rarely lose my temper.
14. I can't say I always keep disruptive impulses in check.	0	1	2	14. I always keep disruptive impulses in check.
15. I can't resist the temptation to say something even when I know it won't help.	0	1	2	15. I resist the temptation to say something when I know it won't help things.
16. When I am upset, I do things I later regret.	0	1	2	16. Even when I am upset, I always take a sober second thought before I say or do things I will regret later.
17. Bad things happen to good people - some people just get all the breaks.	0	1	2	17. I know that I am totally responsible for my successes or failures.
18. I am not very good at thinking outside the box.	0	1	2	18. I am good at thinking outside the box.
19. I don't think I come across as very confident or self-assured.	0	1	2	19. I come across as confident and self-assured.
20. When I am frustrated, I become upset and will brush people off.	0	1	2	20. I can tolerate a great deal of frustration without becoming upset or brushing people off.

Emotional Intelligence Inventory ©

| | Agree with the statement on the left | Agree with both statements equally | | Agree with the statement on the right |

	0	1	2	
21. I don't waste a lot of time trying to under-stand people's feelings, I look at their actions.	0	1	2	21. I try to understand other people so I can get along better with them.
22. My lack of sensitivity to others at times negatively affects my ability to manage my interactions with them effectively.	0	1	2	22. My sensitivity to other people's feelings enables me to manage my interactions with them more effectively.
23. I am not the kind of person that picks up on "vibes."	0	1	2	23. I am sensitive to and pick up on the mood in the room.
24. I am seldom in touch with my emotions.	0	1	2	24. I am always in touch with my emotions.
25. I have difficulty reading people.	0	1	2	25. I can read people like a book.
26. When someone close to me experiences a setback, I seldom come up with a way to help them solve their problem.	0	1	2	26. When someone close to me experiences a setback, I can usually come up with a way to help them solve their problem.
27. I have an urge to flee when people get too touchy-feelie around me.	0	1	2	27. I am very comfortable talking about feelings with others.
28. I am certainly not prejudiced, but racial diversity is very low on my priorities.	0	1	2	28. I am delighted to see more visible minorities in my workplace.
29. I am often at a loss for words when someone else is hurting.	0	1	2	29. I always know what to say to make people feel better.
30. I am not that good at communicating empathy.	0	1	2	30. I show others I care about what they are going through.

Emotional Intelligence Inventory©

	Agree with both statements equally	
Agree with the statement on the left		Agree with the statement on the right

31. I am not the most effective communicator, and I often find my mind wandering when someone else is talking.　　0　1　2　　**31.** I am a very good listener and communicate clearly and effectively.

32. Teaching and coaching are not my forté.　　0　1　2　　**32.** I am a good teacher and coach and can inspire others.

33. I make decisions based on the facts as well as my own opinions.　　0　1　2　　**33.** I always take a collaborative approach to decision-making.

34. I model independent qualities such as determination, problem-solving, personal effort and hard work.　　0　1　2　　**34.** I model team qualities such as cooperation, respect, and enthusiasm.

35. I am not that good at de-escalating conflict and anger.　　0　1　2　　**35.** I can usually de-escalate conflict and anger.

36. When I am under stress or upset, I tend to brush people off.　　0　1　2　　**36.** When I am under stress or upset, I still take the time for other people.

37. I don't try to explain myself to others.　　0　1　2　　**37.** I can explain myself to others well.

38. Salesmanship is not my thing!　　0　1　2　　**38.** People say I can be very persuasive.

39. I don't like teams very much and would rather do my own thing.　　0　1　2　　**39.** I am a good team player.

40. I do not take criticism well and often become defensive when criticized by another.　　0　1　2　　**40.** I listen openly and do not become defensive when criticized by another.

Evaluation

On the following page you will find the emotional intelligence score sheet. Simply add together your responses within each of the ranges indicated and place the sums in the boxes provided.

The Emotional Intelligence Inventory is a normative instrument, that is, your scores are compared to everyone else who has taken this instrument.

The categories described on page 45 may prove useful insofar as they may underscore your strengths, as well as indicate areas for improvement for each of the components of emotional intelligence.

EMOTIONAL INTELLIGENCE ASSESSMENT

A	SELF-AWARENESS

B	SELF-MANAGEMENT

C	SOCIAL AWARENESS

D	RELATIONSHIP MANAGEMENT

```
| | | | | | | | | | | | | | | | | | | | | | | | | | | | | | | | | | | | | | | |
0           5              10             15             20
```

EQ	EMOTIONAL INTELLIGENCE

```
| | | | | | | | | | | | | | | | | | | | | | | | | | | | | | | | | | | | | | | |
0    10    20    30    40    50    60    70    80
```

A	Sum of Questions:	1 - 10	
B	Sum of Questions:	11 - 20	
C	Sum of Questions:	21 - 30	
D	Sum of Questions:	31 - 40	
EQ	TOTAL:	1 - 40	

See Color Plate Appendix A – Page 198

EVALUATION

**SCORE
65 – 80**

OUTSTANDING ABILITY

Your score is well above the norm and indicates that you have extremely good emotional intelligence. This high score may reflect a natural ability or may be a result of continuous efforts on your part to develop your abilities.

**SCORE
48 – 64**

A STRENGTH TO BUILD ON

Your score is above average. It is possible, however, that you did not score above average in each of the components of emotional intelligence. You may wish to examine those areas where you could build on your above-average skills.

**SCORE
32 – 47**

AVERAGE ABILITY

Your score is average. In some of the areas of measurement, you are doing well, however, it is likely that you are subpar in some of the components of emotional intelligence. You may wish to earmark those areas for improvement.

**SCORE
16 - 31**

SUBPAR ABILITY

Your score is below average. This indicates that while you may respond in an emotionally intelligent way in some situations, this is not always the case. You may wish to highlight for improvement those components of emotional intelligence where you scored the lowest.

**SCORE
1 - 15**

WORK IS NEEDED

Your score is well below average. It is likely that your poor emotional intelligence skills are limiting your effectiveness. By improving your abilities in each of the component areas, you will experience a vast improvement in your relationship success.

Chapter 5

Insight and Awareness

I was rereading one of my firm's seminar brochures the other day. The brochure was advertising a working-with-people seminar, and I noticed that throughout the brochure, we spoke time and time again about building trust and rapport in relationships.

It struck me that really these two terms don't necessarily go hand in hand because they're not altogether equal. In order to build true rapport in any relationship, whether in your personal or your professional life, with bosses or with co-workers; with spouses or with children, some level of trust has to exist first.

Many of the failures that we experience in our relationships stem from the fact that there's a lack of trust in those relationships.

The research teaches us that in order for trust to exist in any relationship, three conditions first must be present. In all trusting relationships, we find as a feature of those relationships contingency. In order to experience trust in those relationships, there must be contingency; that is, the person to whom we give our trust must at least be perceived by us as being in a position to affect us or influence our behavior in some important or significant way. Without contingency, there's no opportunity for trust to exist and probably no reason for it to exist.

Secondly, in all trusting relationships, we find as a feature of those relationships the principle of predictability. In order to have trust, we must have some level of confidence in expectations as to the behavior of the trusted person. You can't have trust without predictability. You can have hope. If I'm walking down one of the backstreets of Chicago late at night with a large amount of money in my pocket and I hear noises ahead in the shadows, I may hope that it's a policeman, but that's not the same thing as trusting that it is a policeman.

Finally, in all trusting relationships, we find as a feature of those relationships alternative options, or free will. We all have free will, and for trust to exist, we have to be able to exercise it freely. In other words, you can't compel people to trust you; people have to exercise their free will in a relationship in order for trust to exist.

Now, I know that this is probably as clear as mud, but let me give you an example that may bring some clarity to the role of these three features.

Consider the good farmer who is working on repairing a damaged piece of equipment, let's say a pump at the bottom of a shallow well. His labors take him a period of six or seven hours, and his wife, recognizing the fact that her husband won't be returning for lunch, which is his custom, says to their daughter Susan, "Suzy, would you take this bagged lunch to Daddy at the well site?"

Well, the obedient daughter does as she's told, but when she appears at the site of the well, she can't see her father anywhere, she calls out, "Daddy?"

She hears from the depths of the well, "I'm down here, Suzy."

Suzy walks to the edge of the dark pit and looks down, but all she can see below is the darkness of the well, she calls again, "Daddy?"

Her father responds, "Yes, Suzy, I'm down here, what can I do for you?"

Suzy answers, "I have brought you your lunch!"

Her father shouts back, "Suzy, I've got some grease on my hands. Just toss it in."

Suzy again responds, "But I can't see you!"

Her father shouts back, "I know it's dark down here, but I can see you. Just toss it in."

Suzy walks to the edge of the pit and throws it in, and she can hear her father catch it.

But then her father shouts back, "Suzy, why don't you join me for lunch? Just jump in and I'll catch you." Suzy again looks down the well, but all she can see is the blackness of the hole; however, trusting in the relationship that she has with her father, she leaps into the darkness, and of course, her father catches her.

Then let me ask you this question: What was the contingency in that relationship? Was the father, the trusted person in this instance, in a position to affect his daughter in some important or significant way? Yes. Had the father been negligent in his responsibility or duty to catch his daughter, the child could have been seriously injured. Yes, there was contingency.

Was there predictability? Was the trusting person, in this case Suzy, able to predict her father's behavior in this instance? Yes. Again, had it been a hired hand or other stranger, would she have been as likely to jump?

Finally, were there alternative options available to Suzy? Was she compelled to leap into the darkness? No. Suzy could have done many other things. She could have said, "No, that's fine. I'll walk down the ladder." She could have said, "No, I'll just sit on the edge and talk to you." Or she could have run home to Mother. There were all kinds of alternatives available to Suzy.

The problem with the concept of trust is that, like many other things we will examine here, what works for one person will not always or necessarily work for another.

If you read history or if you read philosophy, consider that there has long been recognition that human beings are uniquely and individually different. We really are like snowflakes; no two of us are exactly alike.

Often at my public seminars, I will flash faces on the screen of well-known but controversial characters such as George W. Bush, President Barack Obama, Donald Trump, Nancy Grace, or Jimmy Swaggart, then I will ask people to write down the first word that comes to their mind when they see these faces flashed on the screen. The result is that there is a wide range of responses from very positive to extremely negative. In fact, I've yet to find one person that everyone unanimously responds to either favorably or unfavorably.

Why do some people see George W. Bush as the Savior of the Western world while others seem to see him as the devil incarnate? Why is it in the United States approximately half the people vote Republican and the other half Democrat?

The fact is that just as some people have different physical characteristics, such as height or weight or gender, so too do they differ in the way that they see things, the way they interpret the world around them, and react to it, as well as a way that they relate to other people.

But there is another message to learn from history and philosophy, and that is that while people may be uniquely and individually different, they also tend to fall into types.

The great physician and philosopher Hippocrates recognized this fact. He spoke about the four temperaments of man: the phlegmatic, sanguine, melancholic, and choleric. He found from his experience that all the people he interacted with tended to fall into one of these four types.

In the tenth and eleventh centuries, the Sufis (a mystical sect of Islam) spoke of the Enneagram, a model that identified three essential types or triads (feelers and relaters and doers) with three personality sub-styles within each.

But the dividing of the human family into distinct types isn't some vague proposition lost in antiquity, somehow attached to the occult and indicative of arcane thinking.

Some of the greatest psychologists of all time, Carl Gustav Jung[12] in particular - have been drawn to the same conclusion. Jung spent a lifetime observing, researching, and analyzing personality, and at the end of his life and career, he suggested that there were four general archetypes or personalities. Jung used different words than Hippocrates to describe his four types; he speaks of sensates, intuitives, feelers, and rational thinkers, but in many ways he was saying the same thing.

Back in the 1970s, another model became very popular in the business community called the "management grid[13]." The research behind the management grid came from Ohio State University[14] and the work they did in their business faculty and school in the 1960s. This model was picked up by a couple of writers and consultants by the name of Blake and Mouton, who popularized this model and found ingenious ways to apply it to almost every occupational group in society.

From the graphic below, we can see that there are two key parameters that the model is concerned with measuring. On the X-axis we have task orientation, and on the Y-axis we have consideration.

The Management Grid
Blake & Mouton

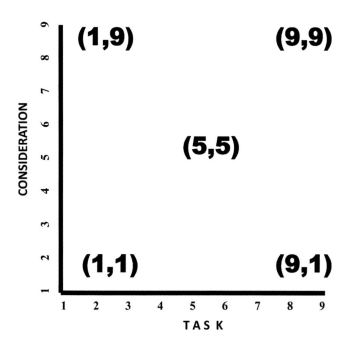

This model suggests that all of us - all people in the workplace are concerned with two key parameters: task and consideration. But we're not all the same; some of us are extremely high or extremely low or in the middle on both. The "management grid" emerges through the unique combination of these two parameters.

The authors would suggest that each one of us is concerned, to a greater or lesser degree in the workplace, with getting the job done.

Some of us are extremely task-oriented; we take the perspective of, "I have a job to do, don't get in my way!" Others are less concerned with task, recognizing that other things are equally important. And some people seem to lack task orientation altogether. They take the perspective that, "If we get this job done today, that's great, if we don't get to it today and do it tomorrow, that's great, and if we don't get to it at all, that's fine as well!"

On the consideration scale, some people are extremely high, very much concerned with the needs and feelings of other people, while other people at the same time seem to lack consideration.

Those towards the top of the consideration scale bend over backwards to accommodate other people. If that other person is hurting, they are hurting. They go out of their way to avoid a scene.

While those in the middle are politically more astute and concerned with the needs and feelings of other people, they view other factors as being of equal importance.

Finally, those people scoring towards the bottom of the consideration scale rarely consider the needs of other people. They make no pretense, and they are never accused of being politically correct. They tell people what they think and let the chips fall where they may.

It is through this unique combination of task and consideration that this matrix-like model emerges. The model suggests that if you can identify where the key actors in your life fall, in terms of their unique combination of task and consideration, then you can explain their behavior and, more importantly, can predict their behavior.

I believe that this is why people find models of this ilk so interesting; they allow us to predict how others will respond to our actions.

Would it not be beneficial to understand how your customers will respond to the offer you wish to advertise before you take the time and spend the money to do so? Would it not be useful to understand how your boss will typically respond to your actions before you take those actions? Would it not be beneficial to be able to understand how your spouse will respond to changes you hope to make in your relationship before you make them?

My own feeling is that the management grid is great as far as it goes, but I think it fails to take into consideration a couple of very important parameters in human personality and management style.

For one thing, the model doesn't speak to the role of assertiveness in the choices made available to you. Were you born or socialized to respond assertively with those around you? I think this is a key characteristic or defining feature of personality. I think this key element must be integrated into any useful or accurate model of personality or management style.

Secondly, the model doesn't speak to the role of emotional responsiveness or emotional expressiveness as a determinant of personality.

The model I am about to present to you, the Behavioral Styles Model, is the best model available for accurate self-assessment, and I feel it also provides the greatest opportunity through its application to enrich the experiences we have with others by developing stronger relationships with them.

The Behavioral Styles Model

Think of a line drawn across a page. At one side of the line (the right side) is written the word "assertive." At the end of the line (the left side) is written the word "non-assertive."

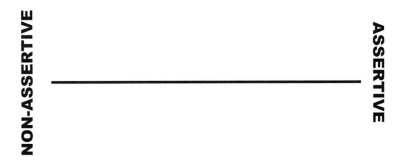

The assertive end of the line indicates a person who is totally assertive in all relationships, at all times, under all circumstances. Clearly, no one would be at this end of the line, the ideal example of assertiveness. Many of us are very assertive individuals, but we're not the ideal example of assertiveness. Nor is there anyone totally at the left end of the continuum, totally lacking any assertive abilities, totally passive, never defends his or her rights, and has the word "victim" stenciled across their forehead. Some of us are non-assertive, particularly in certain social situations, but we're not the ideal example of non-assertiveness.

Now, before we can determine where we fall on this continuum, we have to come up with a definition of what "assertiveness" is. When I ask people at my seminars to define the word "assertive," they typically describe the behaviors of assertive people, and while this approach is useful and altogether appropriate, it's not the same as the definition.

The two key components or parameters of the Behavioral Styles Model are assertiveness and emotional responsiveness.

Assertiveness

If you were to take your pen and draw a horizontal line across a sheet of paper, label the right end of the line "assertiveness" and the left end "non-assertiveness," we would all be found somewhere along this line.

Some of us, by our own nature it would seem, are assertive, and some of us have been educated or socialized to behave assertively. These people would be found on the right-hand side of the line. Others, by their nature (and for reasons we'll delve into later), behave non-assertively or passively in their interactions with other people. These people would be found on the left-hand side of the line.

But what is assertiveness? How can it be defined? When I ask this question at public seminars, the typical responses are the ability to voice one's concern, appearing confident, the ability to say "no" when appropriate, or the ability to take initiative, etc.

I usually point out to the group at this point that what they've given me is not a definition of "assertiveness," but rather they have described the behaviors of assertive people.

We can take one of two perspectives as we try to come to an understanding of human behavior.

We can take a purely psychological approach, in which we try to burrow into the minds of other people and determine what their motivations were, what their intent was. I think this path is very dangerous, to play psychoanalyst. Alternatively, we can take a behavioral approach, the approach most people instinctively take, and speak to observable, notable behaviors.

Below is a list of common, but notable, observable behaviors of assertive people. As we go through this list, think about how many of these characteristics, and to what degree and extent, are representative of your normal behaviors.

Assertive Indicators

Firm Handshake	Strong Opinions
Fast-Paced	Leans into Conversations
Direct Eye Contact	Initiator of Conversations
Risk-Taking	Confrontational
Voice Intonation	Confidence
Decisiveness	Powerful First Impression

Let me elaborate a little on each of these behavioral features:

1. Handshake

    When an assertive individual meets another person, they grab hold, they squeeze, and they shake, whereas when a non-assertive person meets another hand, which is usually extended only in response to the other's initiation, it is more likely to be a touch or light acceptance of the other grip. Now, obviously this is not conclusive or solely indicative of assertive or non-assertive behaviors. Many of us are taught as children that we should always have a firm handshake, but there is nonetheless a correlation between a firm handshake and an assertive personality.

2. Pace

    There is a higher correlation between pace and assertiveness. Generally speaking, assertive people are high-energy, fast-paced individuals. They move quickly from one activity to another. There is animation and motion. The non-assertive person, on the other hand, appears more cautious, with smaller movements, and appears slower in action and behavior.

3. Direct Eye Contact

Clearly, there is a higher level of direct eye contact in the case of the assertive person. When communicating with another, they look that person in the eye, whereas with the non-assertive person, the focus is indirect; they look around at other people, and they simply are more likely to make eye contact more intermittently and, at the extreme, may look away.

4. Risk-Taking

The assertive person takes greater risks, which is observed in terms of their communicating behaviors which are wide ranging and include vocal intonation and modulation; they use their bodies to communicate; they gesture; they move around. The non-assertive person tends to be more static; they speak more slowly and softly and may even speak in monotone. They tend not to gesture or use their bodies to the same degree as the assertive person.

5. Decisiveness

The assertive person is more readily able to make quick decisions; they are not always good, but they are quick! The non-assertive person labors over even the most inconsequential decisions. They tend to be more cautious and careful.

6. Strong Opinions

    The assertive individual tends to express strong opinions vs. mild, tenuous statements. "This is my opinion; this is what I think; this is the truth." The non-assertive person, on the other hand, tends to say things like, "Don't you think that…"or, "Maybe, couldn't it possibly be…."

7. Initiation of Conversation

    The assertive person is more likely to initiate the conversation. The non-assertive person is more likely to defer. "I'm not going to say something until he says something."

8. Confident Appearance

    The assertive person appears confident rather than shy; they confront rather than go along.

Generally speaking, we see the assertive person as powerful and the non-assertive person as friendly or nice.

Look again at the list above. According to these characteristics or this set of criteria, in terms of assertiveness, are you left of center or right of center?

Later in this chapter, I will be asking you to take the Comprehensive Behavioral Styles Inventory (CBSI) that will allow you to accurately determine where you fall on the assertiveness scale, but before we go there, let's complete our model.

Emotional Responsiveness

If you were to take your pen and draw a vertical line bisecting the assertiveness line in the center and label the top of this line "expressiveness" and the bottom of this line "non-expressiveness," everyone could again be found on that line.

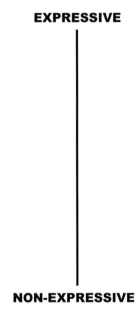

EXPRESSIVE

NON-EXPRESSIVE

Some of us, those of us scoring toward the top of this line, are very much people-oriented. We need to work with and around others; we are good team players; we dislike being alone. Others, on the other hand, would rather work individually on projects; we would rather spend our time individually solving problems than attending meetings or seeking consensus with others.

Below are some of the behavioral characteristics of expressive and non-expressive people:

Expressiveness

Animated Facial Expression	Personable and Open
Use of Gestures	Less Use of Time
Playfulness	Informal Dress Code
Comfortable with Small Talk	Shows Feelings
Decisions Influenced by Feelings	Seeks Contact
Supervises in a Personal Manner	Feelings-Oriented

A little explanation is also required here:

1. Animated Facial Expression

    It is not that difficult to identify an Expressive because their emotions radiate in their countenance. When they're happy, they laugh; when they're sad, it shows; and when someone hurts their feelings, they may say it doesn't matter, but it matters. On the other hand, the Non-Expressive, they may not be stoic, but they are clearly less animated than the Expressive.

2. The Use of Gestures

Expressives tend to use their bodies to communicate. They gesture; they move around. Non-Expressives, in contrast, tend to be more static. Their movements are small and controlled.

3. Playfulness

Expressives appear more playful; Non-Expressives more serious. Non-Expressives are suspicious of those who use humor, particularly in situations where they feel it is inappropriate.

4. Dress Codes

Although far from conclusive, dress codes can also be an indicator of expressiveness. If an Expressive is not sure what appropriate dress is for a given occasion, they will generally suit themselves. If anything, they will err in the direction of informality. In the case of the Non-Expressive, if they are not sure what dress is appropriate, they will typically overdress, moving in the direction of formality.

5. Feelings Orientation

The Expressive also tends to show their feelings, whereas the Non-Expressive tends to hide their feelings. I'm not suggesting that Expressives feel and Non-Expressives don't feel. We are all human beings; we all feel. But in the expression of emotion is a grave difference, and it is partly a function of behavioral style.

6.   Small Talk

Expressives are more comfortable with small talk, with what I call "drapery talk," the kind of meaningless conversational claptrap that acts as a social lubricant. "I like your drapes." "Warm day but humid." "Did you see the football game last night?" Whereas Non-Expressives find it difficult to engage in this type of conversational drivel. They think to themselves, "I've nothing in common with this woman, what am I going to talk about, the weather, the football game, those ugly drapes!"

7.   Decision-Making

Expressives often make decisions based on, and motivated by, their feelings. They may say things like, "I just don't feel right about what went on," or, "My wee small voice is shouting at me," or, "My intuition tells me such-and-such." Non-Expressives are more likely to say things like, "I don't think this is the right course of action," or, "The facts don't indicate such-and-such," or, "The data isn't friendly."

8. Personable and Open

    Expressives appear to be more personable and open to others. Non-Expressives appear more closed and aloof.

9. The Use of Time

    In terms of the use of time, there is a significant difference between Expressives and Non-Expressives. Expressives are more flexible as they approach projects and assignments, being able to reprioritize when necessary. Non-Expressives, on the other hand, become stressed when changing conditions disrupts their plans.

10. Supervision

    In the case of the Expressive, supervision is often done in a personal manner. If they think it might help improve a given situation, they won't hesitate to go out for a drink or out to dinner with the staff to discuss a situation or problem. Not so with the Non-Expressive. They believe in maintaining a "professional distance." They say to themselves, "I'm not going to take them out for a drink. They might start to like me!" These are the people who say, "It's not wise for doctors and nurses to fraternize." "It's not wise for officers and enlisted men to drink together." "It's unwise for management and labor to come together. It's an adversarial world we live in, and people have to know their place."

In essence, Expressives seek contact, emotional contact, with other people. Non-Expressives, on the other hand, are seeking to avoid contact. Expressives are feelings-oriented. Non-Expressives are thinking-oriented.

It's through the unique combination of these two parameters that the Behavioral Styles Model emerges. The model suggests that there are four distinct social or behavioral styles.

Some people are highly assertive and highly expressive; these individuals we will label as Dreamers. In the general population in the United States, they account for approximately 27%.

Some people share the emotional responsiveness of the Dreamer but are less than average when it comes to assertiveness. These individuals, accounting for 25% of the population, we will call Supporters.

Some 23% of the population are assertive and at the same time non-expressive and task-oriented. We will label these people with the title Commander.

Finally, approximately 24% of the population is both non-assertive and non-expressive. We will refer to these as Thinkers.

The Behavioral Styles Profile

The Behavioral Styles Model is both a very simple tool (describing four basic styles), as well as a fairly complex tool, allowing for the fact that no two people are exactly the same.

And herein lies one of its main differentiators from many of the other more common personality profiling tools. Not only will you fall generally within one particular behavioral style, but the model also accepts that you may display different behavioral responses in your various relationships, as well, you will have shades of all four behavioral styles within your make-up, resulting in your inclusion in one of sixteen sub-types or temperaments. So two people of the same basic behavioral style can and do act quite differently.

Behavioral Styles Profile

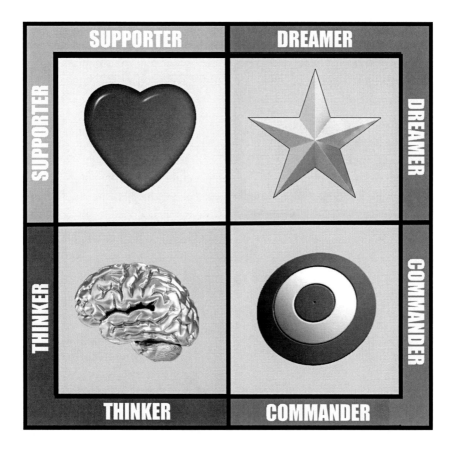

Please See Color Plate – Page 199

There are some of us who are highly assertive individuals but who also like to work with and around other people. We're going to call these individuals "Dreamers." The term is somewhat pejorative, but I will explain in due course why I chose the word "Dreamer" to describe this combination – assertiveness and emotional responsiveness, or expressiveness.

There are some of us who are highly assertive but more task- than people-oriented. These people, while wanting to maintain good relationships with others, will, in a pinch, choose the accomplishment of an important task over the approval of other people. They are assertive and task-oriented. We'll call these people "Commanders."

Some people enjoy social interaction with others very much. They are good team players and work well with other people; however, in terms of assertiveness, they're below average. They will choose relationship success over other types of accomplishments in their lives. These individuals we're going to refer to with the title "Supporter."

And there are some people who are neither highly assertive nor are they people-oriented. They are concerned more with tasks and their accomplishments and are at the same time non-assertive. These individuals we will refer to as "Thinkers."

Before we delve even further into this model, I would suggest to you that the most toxic relationships we could find ourselves in are the diagonals in this model. For example, there is considerable interpersonal stress when Commanders and Supporters try to work together. They have absolutely nothing in common.

Supporters are filled with the milk of human kindness; they are supportive and encouraging to others, they go out of their way to avoid a scene, sometimes giving in even when they know they are right rather than have conflict enter the relationship. They are aware of and concerned with the needs and feelings of other people. They want everyone to experience high levels of self-esteem. The

Commander, on the other hand, takes the, "Damn the torpedoes! Full speed ahead!" approach. They are much more concerned with accomplishment than with relationships.

Likewise, there's a tendency towards conflict or certainly a social uneasiness when Dreamers and Thinkers seek to communicate for the purposes of accomplishing a task or project. The Dreamer manages by the seat of their pants. They possess the "gift of the gab"; that is, the ability to speak with all types of people. While they tend to be effective motivators, they are not detail-oriented and can sometimes be perceived as flighty by other people. It is for this reason that they tend to have difficulty communicating and working effectively with the task-oriented Thinker.

Now, clearly we have conflicts with the people next door, the style adjacent to our own. Dreamers and Supporters have conflicts, as do Commanders and Thinkers; Supporters and Thinkers, as do Dreamers and Commanders, but they are never as great as these diagonals. The reason for this is that in the case of the diagonals, there is no commonality. Dreamers and Supporters are both people-oriented, and they make decisions accordingly. The source of their conflict stems from the fact that one (the Dreamer) will dominate the relationship.

Dreamers and Commanders have assertiveness in common. One will not dominate the other; the conflict comes from differing priorities. The Dreamer's priority is people and relationships, whereas the Commander's priority is task.

Commanders and Thinkers are both task-oriented individuals concerned less with social interaction and the interpersonal niceties than they are with accomplishing the goal or task in both an effective and efficient manner. Over time, the Commander will usually move to dominate decision-making, resulting in hard feelings.

And while Supporters and Thinkers have non-assertiveness in common (meaning one will not dominate the other), their priorities again are really quite different. The Supporter's priority is the maintenance of relationships with others, while the Thinker's priority is problem-solving and goal attainment.

You may have recognized through this discussion that you tend to fall closer to one of these four behavioral styles than the others.

One point I would like you to understand, however, is that we all have elements of each of the four styles within our personality. One is simply more predominant. It is for this reason that our personality seems to differ from one relationship to the next.

The Behavioral Styles Matrix below indicates the relationships between the two parameters expressiveness and assertiveness.

Comprehensive Behavioral Styles Inventory™
360° Emotional Intelligence Assessment

BEHAVIORAL STYLES MATRIX ®

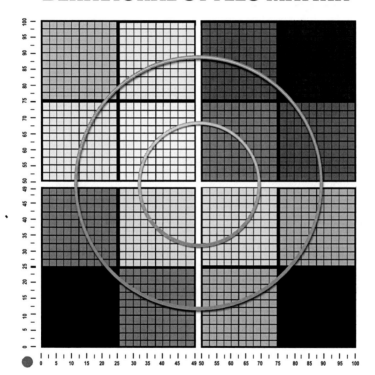

DOMINANT BEHAVIORAL STYLE:

PROFESSIONAL SUB-STYLE:

Color Plate on Page 200

On the next few pages, we will examine the four styles in some detail.

Style Characteristics
The DREAMER

1. Spontaneous

2. Outgoing, Fun-loving

3. Enthusiastic

4. Generalizes – Not Detail-Oriented

5. Exaggerates

6. Seeks Involvement

7. Dislikes Being Alone

8. Works Quickly – High Energy

9. Anecdotal

10. Seeks Self-Esteem and a Sense of Belonging

The Dreamer is spontaneous. They often leap before they look. They have a bias for action. Not big on research or homework, they manage by the seat of their pants. They are responsive and sometimes reactionary.

They are outgoing, fun loving, and enthusiastic. The life of the party, they have the "gift of the gab," the ability to speak with anyone about anything.

This ability to put other people at ease draws others in, encouraging them to communicate, another facility the Dreamer has is their ability to lead others to higher levels of motivation.

Some may, however, perceive them as coming on too strong, monopolizing the conversation, or being too brash.

The greatest single feature of their personality is their enthusiasm. Their enthusiasm is contagious. They can dream and get other people caught up in that dream. That is why I chose the moniker Dreamer to label them.

They are so passionate about their dream, idea, or commitment that they can lead others to share their dream to come on side, to agree with them or vote for them or to sign on the dotted line.

However, they tend to generalize too much, and they are not detail-oriented. They become easily bored, and when they do become bored, they will often jump too quickly from one activity to the next, leaving some tasks undone. They also tend to exaggerate.

The Dreamer seeks involvement with other people. They dislike being alone. They hate budget time, when they are forced to retreat to their own offices for two or three weeks of work on the budget. They will find any excuse to get out of their office and interrupt other people. They simply cannot work on their own for long periods of time without any interaction with other people.

They are anecdotal in their communications and interesting people to be around. They use colorful, expressive language, illustrating points with stories, examples, or parables. They usually have a great sense of humor.

What they really seek is self-esteem and a sense of belonging; what Abraham Maslow[13] called the "ego needs" and "social needs." They want to feel part of a group, but they also want to be recognized; they want to be stroked. They want others to know that they are superior in some way than the group norm.

If we were to pencil in their greatest single skill, we might use the word "persuasiveness." The Dreamer can persuade others to action; they motivate other people to act. This is a powerful skill in organizational life. The ability to share one's vision with others is a key component of leadership.

Their intent is to get appreciation or applause. The symbol might be the star. They want the center stage; they want other people to recognize their talents and their value.

A few examples of Dreamers from popular culture might be comedic actors Jim Carrey and Robin Williams, or comedienne Ellen DeGeneres. Many talk-show hosts come from this quadrant, David Letterman, Jay Leno, Conan O'Brien, and Craig Ferguson are examples. The Dreamer's quick wit and sense of humor make them ideally suited to the world of entertainment.

Sales, marketing, or advertising are other occupations that Dreamers are drawn to. Have you known salespeople imbued with all the strengths of the Dreamer, the ability to motivate other people to action, who can get prospects emotionally involved in the purchase of their good or service?

Perhaps you have also known salespeople guilty of the weaknesses of the Dreamer, who lack detail, who become easily bored - the salesperson that tends to lose their enthusiasm once the sale has been made or fails to follow through on promises made before you signed on the dotted line.

Politics, at least the old-style baby kissing, backslapping, glad-handing politician.

We find accountants coming from this quadrant, as well as engineers, CEOs, and human resource specialists, but we find a predominance of people coming from the world of entertainment, advertising, politics, and sales.

Style Characteristics
The SUPPORTER

1. Cooperative

2. Slow in Action and Decisions

3. Dislikes and Avoids Conflict

4. Seeks Close Personal Relationships

5. Patient, Diplomatic, Loyal, and Dependable

6. Highly Supportive of Others

7. Weak at Goal-Setting and Self-Direction

8. Seeks Security and a Sense of Belonging

The Supporter is more cooperative than the Dreamer. Dreamers need recognition; they need others to recognize their status and uniqueness. Supporters, on the other hand, do not have this kind of ego involvement and therefore tend to be much more cooperative. It does not matter as much to the Supporter that others recognize that their contribution was greater than the contribution of their colleagues. They take the perspective, "As long as we succeed, as long as the team thrives, as long as the organization grows, I'm happy." This focus on "we" rather than "I" leads to a greater level of cooperation.

Supporters tend to be slow in action and decisions, however. Unlike the Dreamer, who is tearing at the bit, with a bias for action, who leaps before looking, the Supporter focuses more on relationships. Rather than moving too quickly to action, they take a sober second thought, ensuring that their actions will not in any way erode their relationships.

Another defining feature of their style is their tendency to avoid conflict wherever possible. They believe that conflict is something that needs to be avoided, not worked through. This causes them endless problems. They find it difficult to say "no," even when others are blatantly taking advantage of them. By avoiding confrontation, pressure spots emerge and remain.

They seek close personal relationships with other people. They don't need a lot of friends, but they need a few good, close friends. Often the relationships they make in high school they maintain for a lifetime. They go to reunions and will stay in touch.

They are patient, diplomatic, loyal, and dependable. They make good friends because they are great listeners. They are always in your corner. This has great utility in modern organizations because it encourages others toward completion.

Their greatest weakness comes from their greatest strength. They are so concerned with helping others accomplish their goals and service their needs, that too often they neglect their own needs and wants. This can lead to unhappiness in their lives, coming to the realization that they take care of everyone else's needs, but no one takes care of their needs.

Their needs are security and a sense of belonging, what Abraham Maslow, in his hierarchy of needs, called the "social" and the "safety needs." They choose safe careers and safe relationships.

Their single greatest skill is listening.

Their intent is to get along, and their symbol might be the heart. They are lovers; they are certainly not fighters. They're drawn to occupations where listening is essential, psychologist, counselor, diagnostic physician, priest.

Some examples of Supporters might be Mahatma Gandhi, Princess Diana, Jimmy Carter, Walter Cronkite, or Katie Couric

Style Characteristics
The THINKER

1. Cautious in Actions and Decisions

2. Seeks Organization and Structure

3. Logical and Systematic

4. Dislikes Involvement with People

5. Prefers Objective, Task-Oriented Work

6. Fact-Oriented Questioning

7. Seeks Security and Self-Actualization

In the lower left-hand quadrant, we have the Thinker.

The Thinker is cautious in actions and decisions. They have to know the rules of the game before they are willing to play. They seek organization and structure - they demand it.

They are fact-oriented and ask a lot of questions, and they seek a lot of data before they feel comfortable moving forward.

They are logical and systematic people. When they do a job, they do it right, the scientific method. They determine and establish all the alternatives, they evaluate each of those alternatives, and then they choose the most critical path to the attainment of the optimal alternative or solution.

Sometimes, however, they are so focused on efficiency that they lose track of effectiveness.

They dislike involvement with people. Simply stated, their single greatest weakness is their inability to work effectively with other human beings.

They prefer objective, task-oriented, intellectual work.

Their greatest skill is their ability to solve problems. They are tenacious in seeking out the best solution. You might give them a problem and forget that you have given them a problem, but they don't forget, they don't get bored, or jump to a less-challenging task; they will hang in until they come up with a solution.

The Thinker's determination to get it right makes them essential to organizational success.

They are drawn to occupations that afford them the opportunity to solve problems and accomplish tasks individually, without major group interaction. Accounting, engineering, and the pure sciences fit well.

Stereotypical examples of Thinkers might be Albert Einstein, Woody Allen, or Bill Gates.

Style Characteristics
The COMMANDER

1. Strong and Independent

2. Firm in Actions and Decisions

3. Seeks Control

4. Pragmatic and Efficient

5. Low Tolerance for the Feelings of Others

6. Works Quickly, Decisively, Impressively - ALONE

7. Seeks Self-Esteem and Self-Realization

The final behavioral style is the Commander. They are highly assertive and non-expressive.

They are strong and independent individuals, firm in action and decisions. When they set a goal, it is hard to dissuade them from the accomplishment of that goal.

Not only do they seek control, they demand it.

They are pragmatic and efficient people, and for them, the end often justifies the means. This leads, at times, to their single greatest weakness, a low tolerance for the needs and feelings of others.

This weakness can erode their overall success and effectiveness.

There greatest skill is their administrative skill, because one of the key functions of management and administration is coordination, and they are good at that. They can make the difficult decisions often required in key organizational positions in a measured, rational, non-emotional way. Their intent is to get it done.

The story goes that Lee Iacocca, who has been credited with Chrysler, used to have a sign on his desk that read "Just Do It!"

Commanders often choose occupations and careers that provide them with power and control - law, medicine, and of course, the military (from which I chose their moniker). Not always successful in middle-management roles, they come into their own in the executive suite. Many entrepreneurs score out to be Commanders.

Some examples of Commanders from popular culture would be Donald Trump, George W. Bush, Jack Kennedy, Adolph Hitler, and Simon Cowell.

Comprehensive Behavioral Styles Inventory

On page 86 you will find the Comprehensive Behavioral Styles Inventory.

The Comprehensive Behavioral Styles Profile (CBSP) is designed to provide you with an accurate assessment of your individual behavioral style and the relative strengths and weaknesses of that style. More than 50,000 people have taken the Behavioral Styles Profile over the past 30 years, the CBSP is both reliable and valid. Statistical reliability assesses the consistency of results across items within a test. The CBSP has a high reliability coefficient. Validity refers to the degree to which evidence and theory support the interpretations of the test. There is ample evidence that the application of its tenets has proven highly effective in real-world applications as well as interpersonal.

The CBSP has been principally developed from the theories and work of the Swiss psychologist Carl Gustav Jung[11] and uniquely combines the latest research in the field of emotional intelligence, including the work of psychologists Howard Gardner of Harvard, Peter Salovey[5] of Yale, as well as John D. Mayer[6], David R. Caruso[7], and Daniel Goleman[8].

Self-awareness, the ability to understand your own behavioral style, is a key factor in effective leadership. A leader is most successful when his or her strongest personal traits are fully engaged. Of equal importance, however, to your leadership ability and personal success is your social awareness; how accurately you can assess the personality and behavioral style of those with whom you must interact. The behavioral styles construct and the CBSP can greatly enhance your skills in both of these vital areas.

Having now outlined in some detail the four behavioral styles, it is time to complete the Comprehensive Behavioral Styles Inventory

(CBSI). This instrument will provide you with an accurate self-assessment.

The questions or statements are meant to be mutually exclusive; they are intended to be the opposite of one another.

Chapter 6

The Comprehensive Behavioral Styles Inventory

Instructions:

The Comprehensive Behavioral Styles Inventory (CBSI) consists of 100 bipolar statements. Please read both statements carefully, then circle the number CLOSEST to the statement that describes your behavior or belief more. For example, if you feel the statement on the right more than the statement on the left describes your behavior or belief, you would circle the 2. If, on the other hand, you find that the statement on the left best describes your behavior or belief, you would circle number 0. Circle the 1 if you feel both statements reflect your personality or belief equally or you find it impossible to answer the question. Please circle just one number per item and answer every question.

Comprehensive Behavioral Styles Inventory[©]
360° Emotional Intelligence Assessment

Agree with the statement on the left ········

Agree with both
statements equally

········ Agree with the statement on the right

	0	1	2	
1. I would rather work individually on a project than work as a member of a team.	0	1	2	1. I would rather work as a member of a team than work alone.
2. Nothing is more important to me than the accomplishment of a goal or task.	0	1	2	2. People and their feelings are more important to me than the accomplishment of a goal or task.
3. To me, getting the job done is more important than being well liked at work.	0	1	2	3. Being well liked and maintaining good work relationships is more important to me than getting the job done.
4. My co-workers would probably rate me as introverted and reserved.	0	1	2	4. My co-workers would probably rate me as extroverted and outgoing.
5. Most often I make decisions at work based on observable facts rather than on my feelings or intuition.	0	1	2	5. Because of my experience, I most often make decisions at work based on my gut feeling or intuition.
6. Emotions should be always governed by reason.	0	1	2	6. Letting someone else witness my emotions makes me feel good.
7. I am not a very intuitive person; I go by what people say, not what they don't say.	0	1	2	7. I am very intuitive and can generally "read between the lines" better than others at work.
8. I would say I am less outgoing and gregarious than most of my colleagues.	0	1	2	8. I am more outgoing and gregarious than most of my colleagues.
9. I do not socialize very much with my co-workers after work.	0	1	2	9. I socialize a good deal with my co-workers after work.
10. I am thinking-oriented.	0	1	2	10. I am feelings-oriented.

Comprehensive Behavioral Styles Inventory©
360° Emotional Intelligence Assessment

Agree with the statement on the left ——

Agree with both statements equally

—— Agree with the statement on the right

11. I am not in touch with my co-workers' feelings.	0	1	2		11. I am very much in touch with my co-workers' feelings.
12. I am logical and rational.	0	1	2		12. I am imaginative and creative.
13. Working with other people is a necessary evil.	0	1	2		13. Relationships are the most important thing; it's what life is all about.
14. I show very little facial expression when communicating with my co-workers.	0	1	2		14. I show a good deal of facial expression when communicating with my co-workers.
15. I have the ability to work patiently on a project until it is completed. Problem-solving is one of my greatest strengths.	0	1	2		15. I need to work with people; I get a little antsy when I work too long on a project individually.
16. I do not really enjoy office parties, picnics or other social functions with the staff.	0	1	2		16. I really like to get together socially with the people I work with.
17. My communication is usually direct, down-to-earth and focused on the task at hand.	0	1	2		17. My communication at work is somewhat abstract and indirect.
18. I think it is more important to be successful than be well liked.	0	1	2		18. Good staff relations are more important to me than being successful.
19. At work, I am more task-oriented.	0	1	2		19. At work, I am more people-oriented.
20. I would rather spend my time doing my own work rather than coaching others.	0	1	2		20. I really enjoy sharing and coaching staff on new tasks, procedures or assignments.

Comprehensive Behavioral Styles Inventory©
360° Emotional Intelligence Assessment

Agree with the statement on the left ⟋   Agree with both statements equally   ⟍ Agree with the statement on the right

	0	1	2	
21. To be honest, I don't encourage my team to participate in decision-making, but if they come to me with an idea, I listen.	0	1	2	21. I encourage my team to participate in decision-making, and I try to implement their ideas and suggestions when possible.
22. When correcting mistakes at work, I don't worry about jeopardizing my relationships.	0	1	2	22. When correcting mistakes at work, I first seek to find a way that will not jeopardize my relationships.
23. When I come to work in the morning, I start by organizing my tasks and activities.	0	1	2	23. When I come to work in the morning, I usually socialize with my co-workers.
24. I don't like interpersonal conflict at work and probably don't handle it all that well.	0	1	2	24. Nobody likes conflict, but I think my interpersonal skills help me to deal with it effectively.
25. My co-workers would probably say I am more task-oriented than people-oriented.	0	1	2	25. My co-workers would probably say I am more people-oriented than task-oriented.
26. My work style is slow-paced and steady, but also persistent and dependable.	0	1	2	26. My pace is rapid at work - I walk, talk and move quickly.
27. I do not establish a particularly high level of eye contact with people at work.	0	1	2	27. I establish a high level of eye contact with people at work.
28. When I have a disagreement with people at work, I often let it go rather than force a confrontation.	0	1	2	28. When I disagree with someone, I tell them so, even though they do not like it.
29. I find it very difficult to say "NO" to the people I work with.	0	1	2	29. I have absolutely no problem saying "NO" to the people I work with.

Comprehensive Behavioral Styles Inventory ©
360° Emotional Intelligence Assessment

Agree with the statement on the left ——

Agree with both statements equally

—— Agree with the statement on the right

	0	1	2	
30. I often feel guilty or anxious when asking others to do things at work.	0	1	2	30. I ask others to do things at work without ever feeling guilty or anxious.
31. I do have a problem accepting a compliment.	0	1	2	31. I have no problem accepting a compliment.
32. I am cautious in my decisions at work; I seldom take risks.	0	1	2	32. I am not afraid to take risks in decision-making at work.
33. I often stop myself from saying what is really on my mind at work.	0	1	2	33. I usually say exactly what is on my mind at work.
34. I am less assertive than most of the other staff.	0	1	2	34. I am more assertive than most of the other staff.
35. At business meetings, I generally speak less than most others in attendance.	0	1	2	35. At business meetings, I generally speak more than most others in attendance.
36. If I feel that my ideas or opinions might upset others, I won't express them.	0	1	2	36. I express my ideas and opinions at work, even though they may upset others.
37. I am not comfortable speaking to a large group of people at work.	0	1	2	37. I am quite comfortable when speaking to a large group of people at work.
38. I am very reticent to voice my disagreement with someone in a position of authority.	0	1	2	38. I feel free to politely voice my disagreement with someone in a position of authority.
39. When making a point, I seldom raise my voice or use my hands for emphasis.	0	1	2	39. I often raise my voice and/or use gestures to make my point.
40. I often "turn the other cheek."	0	1	2	40. I seldom "turn the other cheek."

Comprehensive Behavioral Styles Inventory ©
360° Emotional Intelligence Assessment

Agree with the statement on the left ———

Agree with both statements equally

——— Agree with the statement on the right

Left	0	1	2	Right
41. People often ask me to speak more loudly.	0	1	2	41. People rarely ask me to speak more loudly.
42. I often put the needs of others at work ahead of my own needs.	0	1	2	42. At work, I generally put my needs and goals ahead of the needs of others.
43. I believe in free and open organizations where everyone is encouraged to participate in decision-making.	0	1	2	43. I believe things work better when you have strong leaders who are not afraid to make decisions.
44. I encourage subordinates to question my directives and suggest improvements.	0	1	2	44. I expect my staff to do what they are told!
45. At work, my philosophy is "It's not whether you win or lose it's how you play the game."	0	1	2	45. At work, my philosophy is more "Winning isn't everything, it's the only thing."
46. If I am interrupted at work by a drop-in visitor when I am in the middle of something important, I rarely show my impatience or ask them to leave.	0	1	2	46. If I am interrupted at work by a drop-in visitor, I find it hard to hide my annoyance and will often say something like "I'm sorry, I have to get back to work now."
47. My co-workers would probably say I am more non-assertive than assertive.	0	1	2	47. My co-workers would probably say I am more assertive than non-assertive.
48. My priority is to "Get along."	0	1	2	48. My priority is to "Get it done."
49. I have difficulty expressing my anger or frustration to a co-worker, especially a boss, even if I think it's justified.	0	1	2	49. I am able to express my anger or frustration with a co-worker or even my boss, if I think it's justified.

Comprehensive Behavioral Styles Inventory ©
360° Emotional Intelligence Assessment

Agree with the statement on the left ———

Agree with both statements equally

——— Agree with the statement on the right

Left	0	1	2	Right
49. I have difficulty expressing my anger or frustration to a co-worker, especially a boss, even if I think it's justified.	0	1	2	49. I am able to express my anger or frustration with a co-worker or even my boss, if I think it's justified.
50. I would describe my work-style as warm and people-oriented.	0	1	2	50. I would describe my work-style as action-oriented.
51. I am a loner.	0	1	2	51. I am a people person.
52. I seldom show my true feelings to friends and relatives.	0	1	2	52. I often show my true feelings to friends and relatives.
53. I enjoy analyzing and solving difficult problems.	0	1	2	53. I enjoy working with people more than solving difficult problems.
54. In my personal life, I make decisions carefully and slowly.	0	1	2	54. In my personal life, I am very spontaneous and at times rash in my decision-making.
55. I appear reserved to others.	0	1	2	55. I appear outgoing to others.
56. I am not particularly interested in getting to know more about other people or what makes them tick.	0	1	2	56. My success with people comes from my interest in and willingness to learn about them.
57. I am less outgoing and fun-loving than most of my acquaintances.	0	1	2	57. I am more fun-loving and outgoing than most of my aquaintances.
58. I am uncomfortable saying the words, "I love you" to men, women and children in a feeling way.	0	1	2	58. I am comfortable saying the words, "I love you" to men, women and children in a feeling way.
59. I am thinking-oriented.	0	1	2	59. I am feelings-oriented.
60. I am logical and rational.	0	1	2	60. I am imaginative and creative.

Comprehensive Behavioral Styles Inventory©
360° Emotional Intelligence Assessment

Agree with the statement on the left ——————

Agree with both statements equally

—————— Agree with the statement on the right

	0	1	2	
61. I am a realist.	0	1	2	61. I am an idealist.
62. I show little facial expression.	0	1	2	62. I show a great deal of facial expression.
63. I like small gatherings and prefer the quiet life.	0	1	2	63. I love to party.
64. I am not very tactile and seldom touch other people. I do not consider myself a sensual person.	0	1	2	64. I am quite tactile and consider myself to be a very sensual person.
65. I cannot often tell when a friend is sad.	0	1	2	65. I can always tell when a friend is sad.
66. I am a really bad joke and storyteller.	0	1	2	66. I am a good joke and storyteller.
67. I would prefer to participate in individual sports.	0	1	2	67. I would prefer to participate in team sports.
68. I seldom embrace my parents and children and tell them that I love them.	0	1	2	68. I often embrace my parents and children and tell them I love them.
69. I am direct and business-like with shop clerks, waiters and other service personnel.	0	1	2	69. I am very friendly and kind with shop clerks, waiters and other service personnel.
70. I am not really a very spiritual person.	0	1	2	70. I am a very spiritual person.
71. My friends would probably say I am more task-oriented than people-oriented.	0	1	2	71. My friends would probably say I am more people-oriented than task-oriented.

Comprehensive Behavioral Styles Inventory ©
360 °Emotional Intelligence Assessment

Agree with the statement on the left	Agree with both statements equally	Agree with the statement on the right

72. When asked to do something by a friend while I am already very busy, my first thought is, "How does this fit into my other priorities?" | 0 1 2 | **72.** When asked to do something by a friend while I am already very busy, my first thought is, " How important is this to my friend?"

73. My conversations are more focused on facts and current issues. | 0 1 2 | **73.** My conversations are more focused on personal life experiences.

74. I am not that easy to get to know in new or unfamiliar social situations. | 0 1 2 | **74.** I am very easy to get to know in new or unfamiliar social situations.

75. Nothing is more important than accomplishing your own goals in life. | 0 1 2 | **75.** People and their feelings are more important than personal accomplishments.

76. I have trouble saying "No" to my friends and family. | 0 1 2 | **76.** I have no problem saying "No" to my friends and family.

77. I do not drive particularly fast nor am I all that impatient in traffic. | 0 1 2 | **77.** I probably do drive too fast and am very impatient in traffic.

78. I do not like to speak publicly. | 0 1 2 | **78.** I like to speak in public.

79. If a stranger offends me or infringes on my rights, I seldom make a fuss. | 0 1 2 | **79.** If a stranger offends me or infringes on my rights, I do make a fuss.

80. I tend to be speechless when I am left alone with a person I find really attractive. | 0 1 2 | **80.** When alone with a very attractive stranger, I have no problem speaking with them.

81. When I experience poor service in a restaurant, I seldom complain directly to the server or manager. | 0 1 2 | **81.** When I experience poor service in a restaurant, I let the server or manager know about it immediately.

Comprehensive Behavioral Styles Inventory©
360° Emotional Intelligence Assessment

Agree with the statement on the left	Agree with both statements equally		Agree with the statement on the right

82. In an elevator, I seldom make an effort to talk with strangers.   0   1   2   82. In an elevator, I make an effort to talk to others.

83. I am not assertive.   0   1   2   83. I am assertive.

84. Because of the tension disapproval can produce, I react in a warm and friendly way.   0   1   2   84. When people do not agree with me, I defend my position and try to convince them I am right.

85. I am generally a slow-paced, calm individual.   0   1   2   85. I am a high-energy, fast-paced individual.

86. I avoid too much direct eye contact.   0   1   2   86. I usually look others straight in the eyes.

87. I seldom raise my voice at home.   0   1   2   87. I often have to raise my voice at home.

88. If someone cuts in front of me in a line, I will rarey tell them off.   0   1   2   88. If someone cuts in front of me in a line, I will always tell them off.

89. When my child, spouse or significant other indicates they are in disagreement with me and wish to follow their own path, I support them.   0   1   2   89. When my child, spouse or significant other charts out a course that I disagree with, I will fight to the end to make them see the light.

90. If my neighbors make too much noise, I am very reluctant to say anything.   0   1   2   90. If my neighbors make too much noise, I certainly communicate my annoyance to them.

91. When a friend borrows something from me and forgets to return it, I feel uncomfortable reminding him or her about it.   0   1   2   91. When a friend borrows something from me and forgets to return it, I don't feel uncomfortable asking for it back.

Comprehensive Behavioral Styles Inventory ©
360° Emotional Intelligence Assessment

Agree with the statement on the left ----

Agree with both statements equally

---- Agree with the statement on the right

92. I often stop myself from saying what is really on my mind.	0 1 2	92. I usually say exactly what is on my mind.
93. I would never use intimidation or manipulation to ensure that I get my way.	0 1 2	93. To be honest, I will use intimidation or manipulation to ensure that I get my way.
94. I make up my mind slowly.	0 1 2	94. I make up my mind quickly.
95. I avoid confrontation as much as possible.	0 1 2	95. I confront people I disagree with.
96. I prefer to solve problems in an unrushed environment.	0 1 2	96. I like to be engaged in active and fast-paced activities.
97. In my personal life, my priority is to "get along."	0 1 2	97. In my personal life, my priority is to "be respected and admired."
98. If a friend were to wake me late at night with an unimportant phone call, I likely would not express my annoyance or tell him not to call so late.	0 1 2	98. If a friend were to wake me late at night with an unimportant phone call, I would express my annoyance and tell them not to call again so late.
99. I don't seek greater responsibility.	0 1 2	99. It is in my nature to assume responsibility.
100. I am more passive than assertive.	0 1 2	100. I am more assertive than passive.

Scoring the CBSI

1	Sum of questions 1 through 25	a		E = (a + b)	
2	Sum of questions 51 through 75	b			
3	Sum of questions 26 through 50	c		A = (c + d)	
4	Sum of questions 76 through 100	d			
5	Ep = (Ax2)	Ap = (Cx2)		Es = (Bx2)	As = (Dx2)

Completing the Score Sheet

The following simple steps will enable you to score yourself on the Behavioral Styles Matrix on page 200.

1. Turn to page 86 and add together your circled responses for Questions 1 through 25 inclusive. Enter this sum in the Box marked with a lowercase "A" above. Then turn to page 91 and add together your circled responses for Questions 51 through 75 inclusive. Enter this sum in the Box marked with a lowercase "B."

2. Now add together the "A" and "B" scores you have calculated above and place that sum in the Box marked "E" (A+B) on the right. This is your EXPRESSIVENESS score.

3. Next turn to page 88 and add together your circled responses for Questions 26 through 50 inclusive. Enter this sum in the Box marked with a lowercase "C."

4. Next, turning now to page 93, add together your circled responses for Questions 76 through 100 inclusive. Enter this sum in the Box marked "D."

5. Now add together the "C "and "D" scores you have calculated above and place that sum in the Box marked "A" (C+D) on the right. This is your ASSERTIVENESS score.

6. Next turn to the Behavioral Styles Matrix on page 202. Beginning at the bottom left corner of the matrix (RED DOT), move up the scale a distance equal to your Expressiveness score in Box "E." Make a mark at that location, then taking a ruler or hard edge; draw a horizontal line across the Matrix through your mark.

6. Finally, starting again from the lower left corner (RED DOT), move across the scale a distance equal to your Assertiveness score in Box marked with an uppercase "A." Again, using a ruler or hard edge, draw a vertical line up through the Matrix at your mark.

7. The intersection of the two lines you have drawn indicates your Primary Behavioral Style.

BEHAVIORAL STYLES MATRIX®

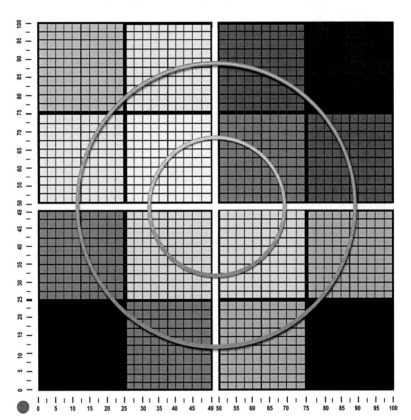

Mapping Your Score

To map your location on the Behavioral Styles Matrix found in Appendix C – Page 200, follow the following four steps:

Step One

Starting from the lower left-hand corner of the Behavioral Styles Matrix (Red Dot), move up the vertical scale to the number you have written in the A (Assertiveness) box on the score sheet. Make a mark at that number on the vertical scale.

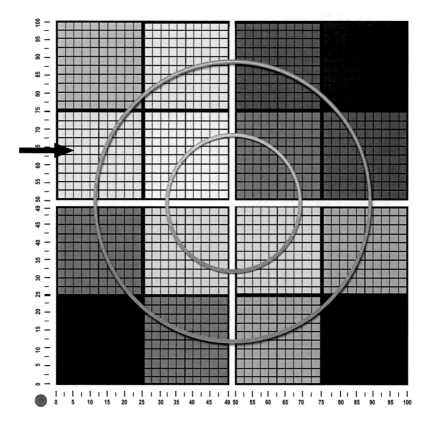

BEHAVIORAL STYLES MATRIX®

Step Two

Next, using a ruler or hard edge, draw a horizontal line across the map through the mark you have made.

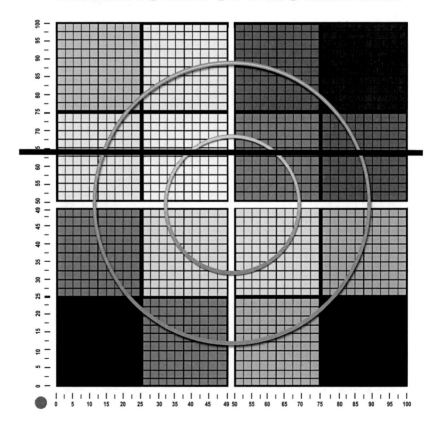

Step Three

Then, starting from the lower left-hand corner (0) again, move across the horizontal scale until you reach your E (Expressiveness) score. Make a mark at this point on the scale.

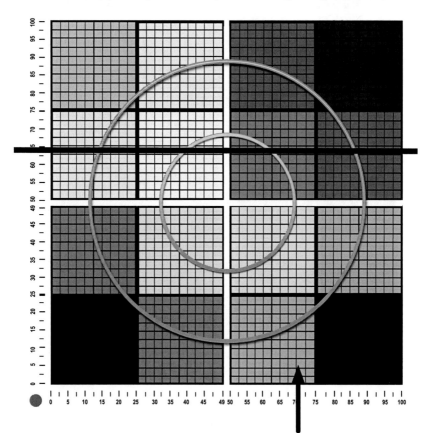

Step Four

Finally, using a ruler or straight edge, draw a vertical line all the way up the page through that mark.

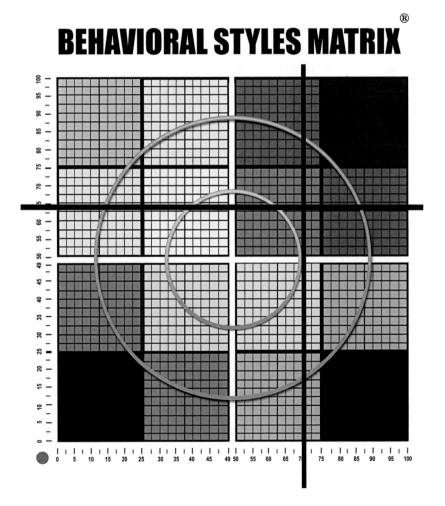

It is the intersection of the two lines that you have drawn that indicates your location on the Behavioral Styles Matrix and your Behavioral Style.

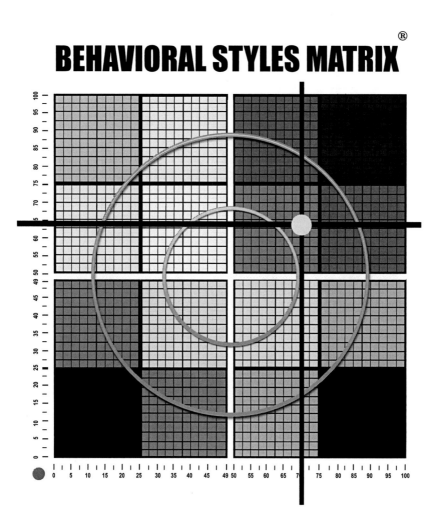

Behavioral Flexibility

The Comprehensive Behavioral Styles Inventory (CBSI) has been carefully normalized. We have tracked tens of thousands of individuals who have taken the CBSI, determining and applying the adjustments necessary to place precisely 25% of respondents within each of the four behavioral quadrants.

As well, your specific location within your behavioral styles quadrant is relevant. The closer you are to the center, the more you take on the characteristics of all four styles.

You will note there are two concentric circles located on the Behavioral Styles Matrix. These concentric circles define and separate the three zones of behavioral flexibility and correlate more or less with one and two standard deviations.

Statistically, 10% of individuals completing the CBSI fall within the inner circle, what I call the "inner circle of flexibility." If you are one of these people, you might interpret this score to mean that you are more flexible than 90% of the population. People, who fall within this inner circle, tend to have less conflict in relationships - at least their behavior and the demonstration of their style tends not to precipitate conflict with others. It's much easier for these individuals to deal with people who fall within the other three styles because they have elements of each of those styles within their own personality.

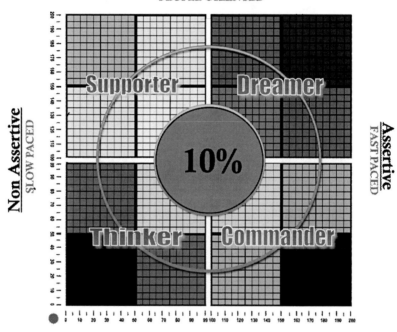

90% of the people who take the test will score in that doughnut area that we might define as falling between the two concentric circles. Most people fall in this range. If you are one of those people, which is likely, the work that we're going to do with this model and an understanding of this model can help you a great deal in understanding why it is that you have particular problems with certain types of people, and it might also give you some insight into how you might improve your relationships with those people by temporarily taking on some of the characteristics of those people.

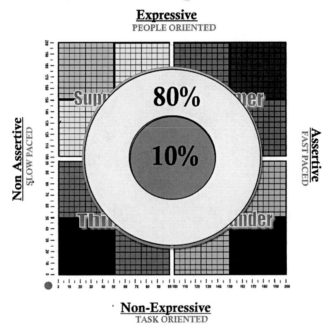

10% of those taking this test will score outside the second concentric circle. This would indicate greater inflexibility than 90% of the population. If you scored in this zone, it does not mean that you're a bad person; it simply means that you're going to be constantly challenged, throughout your life, by those people who are diametrically opposed to you.

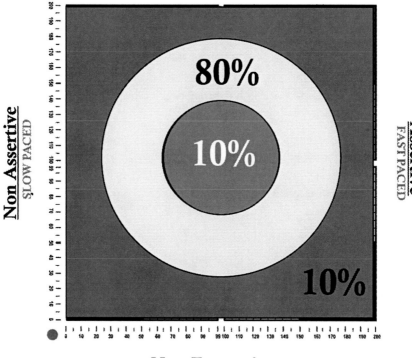

The behavioral styles concept and the strategies for success with people, that you will learn in chapter ten, can help you a great deal to negate this behavioral inflexibility.

It may appear that conflicts arise only with people whose style differs from our own. This is not altogether true, major conflicts can also arise when we communicate, negotiate or otherwise interact with people whose behavioral style is the same as our own.

Two Thinkers working on a project will tend to feed each other's need for ever-increasing detail and data. Two Dreamers may become easily distracted. Two Supporters, wanting to avoid conflict, and not rock the boat may result in commitment to an agreement which they are not really pleased with. When two Commanders come together, the strength of their personalities and their goal and task orientation can get in the way and lead to intransience, if not open combat. They can become like two rams bashing their heads together, neither willing to back down.

I've seen this latter behavior often in the relationship between an administrative professional and his or her boss, both of whom are Commanders. The boss says, "I want you to do this," to which the administrative professional replies, "Not likely," and if she doesn't say it, she is thinking it.

So we can see that there can be interpersonal conflicts with people who are different than ourselves, and there can also be conflicts with people who are very similar to ourselves.

What can be done?

Chapter 7

The Temperaments

Within the four behavioral styles, there are sixteen individual behavioral temperaments. Each temperament has its own unique strengths, weaknesses, and limitations, as well as role preferences. The identification and description of the sixteen temperaments are provided in this chapter.

The Sixteen Temperaments

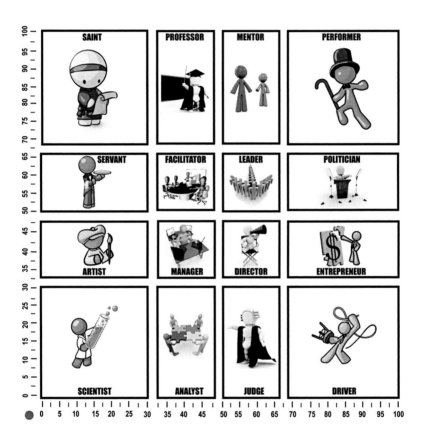

To determine your unique temperament, use the same "E" and "A" coordinates you used to identify your placement on the Behavioral Styles Matrix. You may wish to use the colored version, Appendix D on page 201.

The Four SUPPORTER Temperaments

Within the behavioral style we have labeled Supporter, there are four unique temperaments. While all four combine emotional responsiveness with non-assertiveness, there are nonetheless subtle differences in the way in which these two parameters interface, resulting in nuanced yet significant differences in attitudes, preferences, and behaviors.

The
SAINT

Saints are gentle, compassionate, selfless and kind individuals, concerned and actively involved with the welfare of others. The Saint often put their own needs and goals on the backburner so as to help others achieve their goals or satisfy their needs. They value harmony and are very good listeners. Often the champion of the oppressed and disadvantaged, Saints hold deep convictions. They may become activists for causes they see as important and their unique combination of vision and a desire for social justice can draw others to them for counsel and advice.

The
PROFESSOR

As their name suggests, Professors are thoughtful and somewhat aloof. Their interests are usually more academic than artistic. While more action-oriented than the other three Supporter temperaments., they are generous and loving toward their friends and family. Somewhat enigmatic and hard to get to know, they are often mechanically inclined and can operate equipment well. Paradoxically, while they are willing to try almost anything once, they are somewhat inflexible. They like to do their own thing, which can lead to insubordination, in that they view rules and regulations as limiting their freedom. At times they can be argumentative.

The
FACILITATOR

Often accused of seeing the world through rose-colored glasses, these idealists have a strong personal sense of right and wrong. They work well with others, particularly in team situations. They take a gentle approach to leadership and have an ability to draw on the strengths and talents of others. The Facilitator can skillfully and in a non-directive way, help the group identify common objectives and the best path to their achievement.

This is a highly effective leadership style for information-based organizations.

The SERVANT

As the name suggests, these individuals have a great sense of duty. Rightly or wrongly they feel they cannot personally effect the changes they wish. For this reason they often attach themselves to powerful individuals to whom they are extremely loyal and obedient. Servants are often unappreciated, even though they perform their duties competently. People tend to take advantage of them because of their lack of assertiveness and inability to say "no."

They are not good delegators and would rather just do the task themselves than bother other people with it. Patient, with a deep-seated reserve, they work well alone but can run the danger of becoming invisible.

The Four DREAMER Temperaments

Within the behavioral style we have labeled Dreamer, there are four unique temperaments. While all four combine emotional responsiveness with assertiveness, there are nonetheless subtle differences in the way in which these two parameters interface, which results in nuanced yet significant differences in attitudes, preferences, and behaviors.

The
MENTOR

Great communication skills and the ability to nurture and motivate others make an ideal Mentor. Their ability to understand other people and inspire action evidences their strong leadership abilities. They see value and potential in everyone.

Paradoxically, the Mentor's greatest weakness comes from their greatest strength. They can become easily offended and do not take criticism well. Depression can be an issue, and while they are selfless in raising others to their high levels of achievement, they also expect the appreciation of their tutelage. They have a desire to be affirming of others - and to be affirmed by them. Mentors do well in environments that allow them to serve others with little interpersonal conflict.

The
PERFORMER

Performers love to be center stage. They seek fun and excitement and need to work with and around other people. The life of the party, Performers are great storytellers, and their quick wit and sense of humor leaves a memorable impression on others. They are good communicators, although they tend to be somewhat verbose. Performers cope well with change and are often early innovators. They pay attention to fashion trends and are in touch with the vicissitudes of popular culture. Performers live in the "here and now" and like immediate gratification. This focus on the moment can lead to a low tolerance for rules and established ways of doing things. They multitask well and enjoy the excitement of juggling people and projects. Performers may be viewed as flighty or even lacking depth of character. They tend to get easily bored, and when they do, jump too quickly from one activity to another, often leaving tasks undone.

The
POLITICIAN

The Politician's charm, graciousness, and zest for life make them ideal hosts and hostesses. Their chameleon-like ability leads other people to view them as one of their own, understanding their needs and concerns, believing and feeling as they do. In this regard, the Politician is sensitive to the mood and feelings of others and is attuned to subtle nuances that most people miss. The Politician's assertiveness is tempered by their caring nature and sincere desire to help make the world a better place. They have less of a need to be in charge than the other Dreamer temperaments. Because of their sensitivity, they may overlook facts when they find a situation disagreeable often sweeping problems under the rug.

The
LEADER

The Leader's simultaneous focus on relationships and innovation make them ideal leaders in today's fast-changing world. The Leader's superior communication skills, particularly their ability to persuade, make them strong team facilitators. Leaders enjoy life and are dynamic and enthusiastic. Their empathetic abilities and their genuine admiration of others however, can lead to the loss of their own identity. Leaders are unflappable and open to new ideas. They want others to like them and acknowledge their achievements. Creative and innovative and certainly right-brain dominant, they can and do come up with great ideas, but follow-through can be an issue. Leaders also tend to procrastinate and get easily bored.

The Four THINKER Temperaments

Within the behavioral style we have labeled Thinker, there are four unique temperaments. While all four combine emotional responsiveness with assertiveness, there are nonetheless subtle differences in the way in which these two parameters interface, which results in nuanced yet significant differences in attitudes, preferences, and behaviors.

The
ARTIST

Non-assertive and rather pensive, Artists live in the world of ideas. They are highly creative problem-solvers with an artistic flair. Artists tend, however, to hide their candle under a bushel, not wishing to trumpet their achievements and creations. They have exacting standards and are hard on themselves. Like all Thinkers, they can agonize over decisions. One of the quietest of the temperaments, they need to be alone - often.

The
MANAGER

Managers take time to solicit input and advice from others. This leadership style is particularly effective in team-based organizations. They take a scientific approach to decision-making, evaluating all the alternatives before acting. They like data – the more, the better, and like all the Thinker temperaments, they are slow to act. They urge others to, "Do it right so we don't have to do it again." Time matters to the Manager; however, they may be punctual for appointments but tardy in achieving deadlines. These well-organized individuals have a strong sense of right and wrong and are justly viewed as reliable and dependable.

The
ANALYST

Quiet and reserved, the Analyst tries to make sense of the proliferation of data, converting it into useful information. They are great problem-solvers and have a strong desire to be right.

Analysts tend not to share their ideas and opinions except to those they are the closest to. They are perfectionistic in their outlook and can be their own worst critics, spending a good deal of time second-guessing themselves. Analysts prefer working with ideas than people, and quite rightly do not see meetings as the best use of their time and talents. Analysts are also difficult people to get to know and also have a desire to spend time alone.

The
SCIENTIST

Among the most independent of the sixteen temperaments, Scientists appear more self-confident than the other three Thinker temperaments. Others can mistake this confidence for arrogance. Highly theoretical, their unique combination of intellect and persistence make them powerful problem-solvers. Their need to make things better may leads to perfectionism, as well, their tendency to make decisions unilaterally often leads to conflict. Their Achilles heel is clearly their personal relationships.

The Four COMMANDER Temperaments

Within the behavioral style we have labeled Commander, there are four unique temperaments. While all four combine non-expressiveness with assertiveness, there are nonetheless subtle differences in the way in which these two parameters interface, which results in nuanced yet significant differences in attitudes, preferences, and behaviors.

The
DIRECTOR

Directors are able to temper their assertive abilities with adequate people skills. They can and will make unilateral decisions if they meet with too much resistance on the part of others. They tend to make excellent administrators because of their skills in organization and coordination. Very decisive, they know when enough data is enough.

The most practical of the sixteen temperaments, Directors can make tough decisions and move on without becoming emotionally involved in, or agonizing over, their decision. The Director is achievement-driven and results-oriented. They want more and better. They are high-energy, fast-paced, thoughtful individuals. Their focus is, however, can too often be on short rather than long-term objectives, which can be problematic, at least in some organizational environments.

The
ENTREPENEUR

The Entrepreneur is highly assertive, goal-oriented, and creative, they have big egos, but not out of proportion to their achievements.

Optimistic yet demanding a great deal from their staff and colleagues, they often bring this demanding presence to their personal relationships, which can be highly destructive.

Notwithstanding the above, these individuals are admired and envied by others.

The
DRIVER

The Driver is extremely assertive and the most action-oriented of the sixteen temperaments. They don't suffer fools gladly and can be abrasive and even emotionally abusive. Their fast-paced, no- frills speech and direct eye contact can be intimidating less-assertive individuals.

Drivers are single-minded and have an incredible ability to focus their concentration. They are forthright in expressing their opinions, and as their name suggests, they can be hard taskmasters.

Conflicts emerge as they mistakenly believe that others share their dedication and goal orientation, which they rarely do.

The
JUDGE

The Judge is a high-energy, fast-paced thoughtful individual.

These wise and capable people have the ability to make tough decisions that affect the lives of others rationally rather than emotionally.

It should be noted, particularly in the case of the Judge, that while we describe them as task-oriented, this does not suggest a lack of caring about others, Judges simply approach problems in their personal and professional lives logically.

Not as assertive as the other Commander temperaments, they are still more assertive than average.

Chapter 8

Social Awareness

Before we actually provide the strategies for success with people, it's important to clarify the difference between inferring and observing.

Observing

Behavior is what a person does. It's what others can see and hear. It includes gestures, facial expressions, posture, as well as the words the person uses, and even their voice intonation. Behavior is outside of the person; it's what the world can see.

Inferring

There are many emotions, feelings, and inner qualities operating below the surface that result in the behaviors people observe. Thoughts, attitudes, feelings, beliefs, values, all of these make up the inner qualities of the individual and cannot be observed but can only be inferred. But remember, no one knows for sure what's going on inside another person's head; we can only guess, at best, at what a person is feeling or even thinking.

This is not to say that we cannot thoughtfully and accurately determine another person's behavioral style.

There are four determining characteristics that help us. By assessing how high or low individuals are on each of these major characteristics, we can come up with a reasonably accurate prediction of what their behavioral style is.

Assertiveness

The following four behavioral patterns can be used to assess a person's assertiveness:

1. Quantity of Speech
2. Volume of Speech
3. Rate of Speech
4. Energy Exhibited

Expressiveness

The following four behavioral patterns can be used to assess a person's expressiveness:

1. Facial Animation
2. Voice Intonation
3. Use of Gestures
4. Emotional Inference

Let us first examine each of these four observable behavioral features, or characteristics, of assertive people.

Observable Assertive Behaviors

1. Quantity of Speech

In this discussion, we will consider the target as the individual who we are trying to assess in terms of their behavioral style as the target. Does the target speak often, and is her speech expansive? The more the person speaks and the more often the person speaks, generally the more expressive they are. If a person, on the other hand, speaks very little and typically answers questions in monosyllable, the odds are that that person is assertive. Keep in mind, however, that there is not one indicator in particular that determines a person's assertiveness. We have to look at all four features before assessing how high or low we feel that person might fall on the assertiveness scale.

Remember, too, that a person's familiarity with the topic, as well as comfort level with the material being discussed, will influence the quantity of the conversation. Otherwise, assertive people might defer to others in a group situation when they feel they lack experience, knowledge, or expertise in the topic or subject being discussed. Power structure differences can come into play here, as well as inequities in our structures. An administrative professional, for example, is less likely to speak a great deal at a board meeting to which she's been invited.

2. Volume of Speech

Another indicator of how assertive an individual may be is the volume of their speech. Do they speak loudly, or are their communications soft and tentative?

There's clearly a correlation between the volume of a person's speech and assertiveness.

I think we need to recognize, as well that there is a cultural bias at play here. Cultural differences certainly come into play. Years ago I had an opportunity to work with the Dene Nation in the Northwest Territories in northern Canada. I noticed that very often the Chief was, at least from my perspective, fairly non-assertive. There was very little eye contact, and he didn't speak as much as the other participants in the meeting. When he did speak, it was softly. I asked one of the senior participants in the group why that was the case, and he explained to me that in Native culture, it was rude to look directly at someone or attempt to dominate the conversation.

3. Rate of Speech

Generally speaking, and taking into account cultural differences, the assertive person speaks more rapidly than the non-assertive person. It's been observed, and no doubt is true, that people from the South speak more slowly than people from the rest of the country. But overall, cultural differences aside, people who speak more rapidly tend to be more assertive.

4. Energy Exhibited

The last feature or behavior that you want to observe is the energy expressed in conversation, the level of enthusiasm or passion that the speaker communicates. The assertive person tends to use their body more to communicate a gesture; they move around and use a higher level of facial expression typically when they are communicating. The non-assertive person, on the other hand, tends to demonstrate less energy across the board in their communications. Their tentativeness is generally reflected in a less-energetic approach to communication.

A thoughtful assessment of these four measures will generally give you a reasonable assessment of where the other person is found on the assertiveness scale.

Remember, too, that it is a question of degree, and people don't really fit neatly into four distinct boxes.

If, however, these four dimensions would suggest to you that the individual is more assertive than average, then by virtue of this fact, you've eliminated two of the behavioral styles - Supporter and Thinker.

Next let's evaluate the target's behavior in terms of expressiveness. The following four features help in this regard:

Observable Expressive Behaviors

The following four observable behavioral features or characteristics indicate expressive behaviors:

1. Facial Expression

    The Expressive's feelings are written on their face. They find it very difficult to hide their true feelings. When they're happy, they laugh, and it's typically loud laughter rather than a short, controlled giggle. Their eyes truly are mirrors to their emotions. Expressives have been known to grimace when presented with an unpleasant comment or distasteful story.

2. Voice Intonation

    As the Expressive seeks to communicate their feelings, you will witness intonation of their voice. It will rise and fall and sometimes break. This emphasis speaks to their passion or feelings on issues.

3. Use of Gestures

Expressives tend to use their bodies to communicate. In addition to voice intonation, they will use their hands or arms to form gestures for emphasis. They tend to move around as they speak. They often make large, expansive gestures to illustrate the importance of what they are saying.

4. Emotional Inference

As before mentioned, it's risky to try to draw inferences as to what someone is feeling based solely on observable behaviors. The behavioral approach, which focuses singly on observable behaviors, is a much safer and, generally speaking, more accurate way to go. However, your tendency to want to draw inferences on the basis of clues Expressives present is, in itself an indicator of their emotional responsiveness. Their facial expressions, animation, and types of information they disclose in their speech, as well as their use of gestures, lead us to speculate on their feelings.

These four indicators then form the basis of a reasonable assessment of Expressives. If an individual scores high on all four, or even the majority of these, we can be reasonably confident in predicting that that individual is expressive. In such a case, we have then eliminated the Thinker and Commander. As we then look at assertiveness, we can eliminate one of the two remaining styles.

Likewise, if we find our target displays few of the four broad characteristics associated with expressiveness, we can eliminate Supporter and Dreamer as we look next to the assertive behaviors.

Only when we have given careful thought to the likely behavioral style of the target can we apply the following behavioral strategies for success with other people. When we apply the principles behind the strategies, we are applying the spirit of the Golden Rule.

Chapter 9

Influence Strategies

The Golden Rule

What is the Golden Rule? Well, if you grew up in a Christian tradition and attended Sunday school as a child, you probably think, "Do unto others as you would have them do unto you," when you hear reference to the Golden Rule, although you will not find those words anywhere in your Bible.

The New Testament text that is paraphrased above is Matthew 7:12:

"Therefore all things whatsoever ye would that men should do to you, do ye even so to them: for this is the law and the prophets."

A wonderful principle, an unassailable truth, but what does the last sentence of the Golden Rule mean, "for this is the law and the prophets?" St. Matthew is of course quoting the words of the Lord Jesus Christ. But to whom was Christ speaking?

He is speaking to His people, the Jews in Jerusalem and environs, expressing to them the importance of applying this beautiful principle in their lives, and in particular in their relationships with one another. But He wasn't presenting this information to these people for the first time. He was reminding them that they were taught this principle in the synagogue from the time they were small children.

I mention this to remind the reader that the Golden Rule is not solely a Christian principle, clearly, it's an important tenet to those of us who are Christian, but this truth has been revealed to all people of faith.

In every major religion in the world, you find what we call here the Golden Rule:

Judaism

"What is hateful to you, do not do to your fellowman. This is the entire Law; the rest is commentary."

Talmud, Shabbat 3id

Islam

"No one of you is a believer until he desires for his brother that which he desires for himself."

Sunnah

Confucianism

"Do not do to others what you would not like yourself. Then there will be no resentment against you, either in the family or in the state."

Analects 12:2

Buddhism

"Hurt not others in ways that you yourself would find hurtful."

Udana-Varga 5,1

Hinduism

"This is the sum of duty; do naught onto others what you would not have them do unto you."

Mahabharata 5,1517

Sikhism

"As thou deemest thyself, so deem others."

Kabir's Hymns, Asa 17

Bending the Golden Rule

So we can see the Golden Rule, as we call it, is a universal principle, a truth manifest to all people.

If we were to practice this beautiful principle, not just as individuals but also as nations, many of the problems that we have in the world at the present time might disappear.

But if we practice the Golden Rule too rigidly or strictly in our interpersonal communication, there is a danger that we might fail to achieve the goal we had in mind. Why? Because not everyone always wants to be "done onto as you do!"

In other words, the application of the Golden Rule verbatim might be highly effective if the other person's style is very similar to your own but less successful if they have a different behavioral style.

Rather, if we apply the spirit of the Golden Rule to our interpersonal relationships and interactions with another person, we seek first to take into consideration the behavioral uniqueness of that person.

The following behavioral suggestions are independent of your particular behavioral style. Whether you're a Dreamer, Thinker, Supporter, or Commander, these principles and practices are appropriate. These are best practices for building rapport and interpersonal success with other people.

Having said that, however, their adoption in practice will be more or less difficult depending on your particular behavioral style and how much it differs from the person with whom you're trying to interact.

Strategies For Success With Others

Behavioral Strategies
DREAMER

Strengths:

One of the greatest strengths of the Dreamer is their ability to move others to action through their enthusiasm and playfulness. They possess above-average persuasive skills and feel comfortable speaking with almost anyone. They are fun people to be around, exhibiting great flexibility and an ability to adapt to changing conditions.

Weaknesses:

At times the Dreamer can come on too strong. To some, the Dreamer's playfulness and spontaneity may be seen as evidence of insincerity, unpredictability, and even unreliability. They are allergic to detail and tend not to follow through on tasks, which seem to them boring, repetitive, or requiring solitary action.

Strategies:

1. Support Their Future Orientation

Try as best you can to support the future-oriented approach taken by the Dreamer. Dreamers live in the future, not in the present, and certainly not in the past. They dream big dreams. They can visualize themselves in the future and often see themselves as heroes in their own plays. You may feel that this future orientation is unrealistic, whimsical, or, let's face it, even a little flaky. But try not to communicate your doubts or suspicion. Don't burst their balloon if you want a good relationship with them. Support their future-oriented approach as best you can. Suggest, perhaps, some areas that might be problematic but they need to consider. But by saying such things as, "That's insane, do you really think that could ever happen?" or, "Right, like you could ever really do that," you're chipping at the heart of who they are.

Don't be like the mother whose daughter is uncertain as to what her career choice should be and who jumps from one possibility to another like a bumblebee from flower to flower. The daughter returns home to inform her mother that she has now decided she wants to be a writer, to which the mother responds, "Writer? You can't even write a letter!"

Don't close the door to communication by forcing your perception of reality on them.

2. Don't Engage in Argument

Try not to engage the Dreamer in argument. When the Dreamer is under pressure or stress, their backup style is to become defensive. If you tear a strip off the young salesperson for not doing their job, what response can you expect? Are they likely to respond, "You're right, I'm sorry, I'll try harder." No. You're more likely to hear, "Who are you to tell me I'm not doing my job? You sit in the office all day - I'm out in the battlefield! You don't know what it's like out there, it's a jungle out there."

You have to find another way to communicate with the Dreamer. This does not mean we need to walk on eggshells with the Dreamer, but try to be less confrontational with this style.

3. Build Personal Rapport

Although we could say the same thing for all of the styles, it's even more pertinent when referring to Dreamers. We need to take time to build personal rapport with them. You'll have much greater success with Dreamers if they feel you're in their corner, that you like them, that you accept them and understand what their strengths are and what their value is to the organization. In conducting an interview with a Dreamer, for example, I would begin with a brief discussion of their personal life, perhaps questions about their family or inquiry into areas of interest to them. A little flattery thrown in their direction doesn't hurt. Offer a congratulatory observation on a recent success or achievement, or a personal compliment. This can be taken, of course, too far. I've seen examples in organizational life where, after twenty minutes of friendly preamble, the interviewer begins with, "Well, what the hell's the matter with you?"

4. Match Their Pace

Try to be fast moving and entertaining. This is called pace and can be applied equally to all of the styles. You want to try as best you can to project the same energy level of the target. Dreamers are generally fast moving, direct, open individuals, you should likewise be deemed to be fast-moving, open, and direct with them. If you moan on and on about some issue or situation, you will lose them. They will tune you out. Find another channel. Therefore, try to make short, unambiguous statements. Ask short and direct questions. Move quickly from one item to the next, and don't be afraid to exercise your sense of humor.

5. Use an Opinion-Based Approach

Don't hesitate to use opinion-based information and decision-making. What is opinion-based information? The simple answer is the use of a testimonial. Where do we see a lot of testimonies being borne today? In court? In church? Certainly. But we find even more testimonies being borne on television or newspapers or periodicals. "Johnny fell in the mud, and his clothes are ruined. But I threw them in the washer with Tide, and now they're like brand new!"

"I've lost 30 pounds with NutriSystem, and I've never felt better!"

Marie Osmond

6. Follow Up in Writing

Follow up any important verbal communications with something in writing. Dreamers are not detail-oriented individuals, and while they may know at the end of a discussion what was discussed and decided, a week from now, a month from now is another story. For that reason, it's important to send something in writing if the issue is important. You'll avoid the later discussion, "You never told me that."

If I conducted a disciplinary interview with the Dreamer, I would follow up that discussion by sending them a memorandum stating something along the lines of, "As you know, it was discussed in our meeting that your behavior was unacceptable in the following ways, and the following changes are required, within the following time frame."

This is one of the reasons why I suggest to clients that minutes should almost universally be kept of management meetings.

7. Compliment the Dreamer Personally

I'm not advocating giving hollow compliments, but in the case of the Dreamer, it can help facilitate the rapport that we spoke to previously. In the case of the Dreamer, if you seek to compliment, don't compliment what they've accomplished, don't compliment how they think, and don't even compliment how they get along with other people - make it personal. "I like the way you look." "What pretty children you have." "You kept me spellbound when you told that story about Mount Everest."

8. Don't Burden Them With Details

Try not to discuss too much detail when you're presenting an overview of the project or discussing policy. The detail can come later. The Dreamer has no problem jumping from one topic to the next; in fact, this could be one of their weaknesses. For that reason, it's best for you to deal with one issue at a time and be somewhat linear in your approach, rather than free form.

9. When Delegating, Ensure Understanding

Make sure the Dreamer has a clear understanding of what it is that you expect. The only way to know if they do have a clear understanding is to ask questions. Ask them to speak back in their own words how they interpret the assignment. There's reluctance on the part of many people to do this because they feel that, "I just told them in plain English. Of course they understand." You can be amazed just how far their interpretation of your message is from reality.

10. Discipline in a Timely and Precise Manner

When disciplinary action is required in your dealings with Dreamers, try to do so in a timely manner. One of the most demoralizing things you can do in your interactions with the Dreamer is to wait for performance-appraisal time to highlight difficulties.

If you're having a problem with the Dreamer, approach them quickly and directly. "I'm only giving you a three this year on cooperation, because you remember what happened last year."

As well, call a spade a spade, let them know in certain terms what the problem is or what you expect from them. Don't make them guess. Don't assume they must know. They may not know, as they see things differently than you do. Therefore, as much as is possible, be direct in your communications with Dreamers to ensure a meeting of the minds.

If you can internalize specific behavioral approaches in your interactions with Dreamers, you will have greater success communicating and negotiating with them. You'll find with certain specific Dreamers in your life, some of these steps will work better than others. You'll also find that with some practice, you will become more proficient in their application.

Behavioral Strategies
SUPPORTER

Strengths:

The Supporter's greatest strength comes from their ability to get along with others, as well as the power of their relationships. They are very loyal and trustworthy, which makes them great team members. They demonstrate a willingness to accept direction.

Weaknesses:

At times the Supporter's concern with strengthening the relationship gets in the way of accomplishing the goal or task. They tend to be slow in both action and decision-making because they are so sensitive to the needs and feelings of others.

Strategies:

1. Take Time to Build Personal Rapport

This point was significant when discussing the Dreamer, and it is also important for the Supporter. In fact, this step could be applied to all the styles, although less significant in your interactions with Thinkers and Commanders.

2. Show a Personal Interest in the Supporter

We take the rapport building a step further in the case of the Supporter. Try to express and demonstrate an interest in the Supporter. They seek in their lives to have the acceptance of other people. It's important for them to feel that you're on their side, in their corner. Give this support unconditionally to them, and you'll generally be pleased with the payoff. In dealing with problem areas, try to separate the problem from their persona. One way to show personal interest is to ask questions about their relationships and family life. Try to notice changes they have made to their appearance, style of dress, etc.

3. Let Them Know You Are Listening

The Supporter wants to be heard. The way in which they communicate doesn't usually convey to other people the message, "I want to be heard." But they do. Let them know you're listening to them. One way to do this is with nodding your head or paraphrasing. I remember the first time I saw myself on videotape responding to a question in the audience, where the camera was trained solely on me and not on my audience. I noticed how often I nodded my head to comments made by members of the audience or offered short, verbal acknowledgements, such as "Yeah, yeah." When viewed out of context, this seemed annoying, even absurd. But the truth is, it's highly functional. In a room full of several hundred people where someone is in the back making a comment, if you were to glare at them like Norma Desmond, they're more likely to cut their comment short, not fully expressing their view. Nodding in encouragement will draw that person out.

Examine the behavior of good interviewers: Larry King, Barbara Walters, or even talk-show hosts David Letterman, Conan O'Brien, or Craig Ferguson. When the guest is speaking, the interviewer or host is often nodding.

When Johnny Carson was the host of "The Tonight Show," they would seldom show Johnny and his guests in the same frame. Why? Because as the guest was speaking, Johnny was constantly nodding his head to encourage that person to complete their thoughts or expand their story.

If you're old enough to remember the Merv Griffin program, you always knew Merv was present, because as the guest was speaking, you could hear in the background, "Yeah, yeah, yeah" coming from Merv.

This principle is particularly important in dealing with Supporters because it communicates to them, "I'm listening to you, go on."

4. Discuss Feelings As Well As Facts

There will be times when you disagree with what Supporters say. The way in which you deal with this discord can have a significant impact on the relationship you will have with them. When you do disagree with a Supporter, discuss feelings as well as facts, but remember that the Supporter lives in the world of feelings. Feelings matter to them. If you keep hammering them with, "Face the facts," you will lose them. Take time for feelings and say things like, "I'm sure you feel that this won't work, but I think I can change your mind," or, "I'm sure you're feeling betrayed by this, but I might be able to help." If you also express how you feel about a particular issue, it will facilitate communication.

5. Set Specific Consultative Goals

Remember we said one of the greatest weaknesses of the Supporter comes from one of their greatest strengths. They are such kind, concerned, and caring individuals that too often they involve themselves in other's goals at the expense of their own.

If you have a Supporter son or daughter who comes to you for counsel and advice on a career choice, you might respond as any parent would, "You choose whatever you want, dear, and you know I'll support you." Sounds nice, but it is absolutely useless.

Yes, it's their decision and it's their choice, but you have to get more involved with them in helping them formulate their own ideas in order to make the correct decision. You need to lead a discussion of their skills and abilities and strengthen their weaknesses and their likes and dislikes. You need to help them identify what the options are and what price has to be paid to accomplish each of those alternatives. Help them lay it out like a banquet.

6. When Delegating, Seek Group Commitment

When delegating to the Supporter, it can serve both you and the organization to obtain a commitment on their part in a group context. Relationships matter to Supporters. If they commit to a project at a group meeting rather than at a one-on-one meeting in your office, they're more likely to follow through. It's one thing to let you down;

it's another thing to let the team down. Use this principle to your advantage when supervising Supporters.

7. Compliment Their People Skills

One of the Supporter's greatest strengths is their ability to get along well with other people. They are peacemakers, facilitators. They encourage other people to express themselves. Compliment this strength and ability.

8. Motivate By Focusing On Relationships

In seeking to motivate the Supporter, it is important to recognize the value they assign to their relationships and the way in which others perceive them. Monetary incentives or increases in power do not work as well to motivate Supporters as it does with some of the other styles. Find ways to allow Supporters to serve others, the group, or the team.

9. Separate Conflict From Their Persona

When disciplinary action is necessary, it's important to separate the conflict from the Supporter's persona. It's one thing to talk about their behavior and quite another thing to talk about their being. When conducting a disciplinary interview with the Supporter, I might talk about coming in late as being inappropriate behavior or missing meetings as being a problem behavior, but when you say things like, "You're irresponsible when you come in late or miss meetings," you have evaluated them as a person.

Like it says in the Bible, we should damn the sin and not the sinner, keep this in mind in your dealings, particularly when dealing with Supporters.

Behavioral Strategies
THINKER

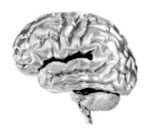

Strengths:

The Thinker's strength comes from their precise, systematic, efficient, and well-organized approach. They have superior problem-solving skills and are perseverant and tenacious. They will doggedly stay with a problem long after others have given up.

Weaknesses:

The weakness of this style comes from their strength. Because they are so task-oriented, they may neglect the emotive needs of those around them. Thinkers are often described by others as being too focused on technology, or picky and humorless.

Strategies:

1. Support Their Thoughtful, Organized Approach

At times Thinkers tend to go on too long. They provide too much detail and analysis. And certainly it's important to move them along, but be careful that you don't rush them to the point where you lose out on some of the organized, thoughtful insight that arose out of their careful analysis.

Recognize that Thinkers only have one way of doing a job, and that's perfectly. But sometimes perfection is too costly; sometimes perfect takes too much time.

2. Convince Them By Actions, Not Words

Thinkers need to be shown. Thinkers are more impressed by action than by words. They have to be shown. I've had many administrative professionals tell me stories about how they tried to convince their Thinker boss to give them added responsibilities to allow them to take on a task or project that freed up their Thinker boss' time, only to be the recipient of all kinds of excuses and reasons and rationales why they should not be given that added responsibility.

My advice to those people is usually to take the bull by the horns and find a part of that project that you know you can do and do perfectly, then do it and bring it to them and say, "See, I did this for you, and I can do it every time." You're more likely in that situation to find your Thinker boss responding, "Okay, carry on for now." But if you wait for them to come to you, you might wait forever, your career can't afford that kind of a wait.

3. Do Your Homework

If you're going to have a meeting with the Thinker, do your homework. Make sure you know the facts ahead of time. In your preparation, give some consideration to the alternatives and the relative advantages and disadvantages of each alternative. Keep an open mind. But help them to do their job by keeping an open mind and understanding what the key issues are.

4. Tell Them the Whole Story

Tell them the whole story. In order for them to do what they are best at (solving the problem), they need all the facts, but present only the facts that would lead to their selection of the alternative you favor.

Many years ago, I was involved as a consultant to a major computer company when they introduced their first-generation PC computer. My job was to help train the sales force in the marketing of these microcomputers. The company's research indicated that the two key areas in the economy that were at that time buying microcomputers for business use were consulting engineering firms and accounting firms.

I was able to convince the sales force that most accountants and engineers were Thinkers, not all, but most. The point I made to them was when trying to sell to a Thinker, you have to provide them with all the facts and as much information as you can that is relevant to their decision-making. I suggested to the salesman and saleswoman that they should present all the advantages of their particular product, but then also in the same discussion highlight all the disadvantages to the equipment.

As you can imagine, this was met with a great deal of resistance and cynicism. "Why on earth would we tell them what the disadvantages are?" The answer was that they're going to find out anyway. These are Thinkers. They are analytical. They will look at everyone's literature that you and the competition leave behind. And make no mistake, they are not impulse buyers. Before they make their decision to purchase, they'll be well versed on the relative strengths and weaknesses of each company's product. If you highlight the advantages of your product and ignore the disadvantages, it's going to negatively affect you and your company because it makes you look untruthful or deceitful, or at the least, manipulative. Will that help you sell anything? I don't think so. We tried this approach, with great success.

5. Follow Up in Writing

I mentioned this before when we spoke about dealing with Dreamers, but I suggest it again for a totally different reason. In the case of the Dreamer, we suggested that by putting it in writing, you avoid arguments and confusion. In the case of the Thinker, we suggest putting it in writing because it doubles the impact of your message. The written word has greater efficacy on the lives of Thinkers than the spoken word. If you sent the Thinker a memo, they'll read it, they'll file it away, it will strengthen your message. Send the same message to the Dreamer, and they may lose it. In the case of the Dreamer, the written communication was as much to help us as it was to help them. But in the case of the Thinker, written communication will strengthen and confirm the message.

6. Don't Rush Them

You can't rush the Thinker. Yes, there are ways in which you can push them for a decision "by 2 o'clock today," but they'll often renege on it when they've had a chance to think.

Also, try not to drop things on them at the last moment. Focus on your own planning to the extent that you can give them adequate preparatory time for thought and analysis.

7. Appeal to Their Need to Be Right

To motivate the Thinker, appeal to their need to be right and to be accurate. Remember that is their intent, to get it right. Sell your suggestions by making them more "right" than they are "right now." If, for example, I were trying to sell a computer to a Thinker, I wouldn't use testimonials, and I wouldn't talk about what so-and-so thinks about this particular product or how, from their perspective, it's the greatest thing since sliced bread. Rather, I would inundate this Thinker prospect with facts and statistics. I would show them in black and white how much more accurate they can be than they are right now or how much more rapidly they can have the information they need to make a decision, a better decision - than they could make absent this product.

8. Compliment How They Think

Compliment the way they think. Their greatest strength is their ability to deal with complex problems and effect thoughtful, intelligent solutions. Let them know that you honor this ability that they possess. Let them know how important this is to the success of the organization.

9. Answer Their Questions

When you give a Thinker an assignment, they will have a lot of questions. Take time to answer these questions, even when you might feel their questions are irrelevant and immaterial. It is by answering their questions that you provide the structure that they long for, the structure that they need in order to move forward.

10. Be Specific When Seeking to Correct

When disciplinary action is necessary, when the behavior of the Thinker is unacceptable, communicate to them directly what the problem is and how this subpar performance impacts the organization or the project at hand. Tell them how specifically their behavior has to change and within what timeframe it has to change, and also let them know that you will be checking to make sure that their behavior has changed. People often suggest this is being a little patronizing, and perhaps it is, but it is not seen as patronizing by the Thinker; it is simply providing the structure they need in order to accomplish the task.

Behavioral Strategies
COMMANDER

Strengths:

The Commander's strength is found in their ability to work rapidly and decisively, alone. They are both assertive and results-oriented. They can generalize well from detail while keeping their eye on the big picture and the bottom line.

Weaknesses:

Commanders may appear at times blunt and abrasive or too focused on the present.

Strategies:

1. Acknowledge Their Accomplishments

The Commander is goal-directed and driven. They are most proud of their achievements and accomplishments. They may be, and often are, self-deprecating, but don't be misled. They are very proud of their achievements, and it is wise to praise them for their accomplishments.

2. Argue the Facts

The worst thing you can do with a Commander is show emotion. They don't want it, and you don't need to show it. Build your case in a logical, measured way, focusing on the facts.

3. Provide Actions and Alternatives for Decision-Making

Do what in the military is called "completed staff work." If a major goes into the general's office and says, "We have a problem. What do you want to do about it?" That is probably the last day you will be a major! You are trained in the military to do completed staff work. You are taught to do some thinking of solutions before you highlight solutions. You are trained to go into the boss' office and say something like, "Boss, we have a problem, and as I see it, there are three solutions, and for this reason and that reason, I think this is the optimum solution, and I have set it up in a way that if you say 'go,' we can do it today."

To which the boss may reason, "Go!" Or the boss may respond, "No, I think for this reason or that reason, this alternative is the best solution." Or the boss may say, "No, there is something you have not thought of, and I think this is a better solution." But at least the major has done his or her thinking.

If you work for a Commander, as many administrative professionals do, then get in the habit of presenting that person with solutions – not problems. They have enough problems.

4. Give Them the Bottom Line and Get Out of Their Way

Commanders are highly responsible, task-oriented individuals. You do not have to spend time attempting to motivate them. Tell them what you need, give them the tools they need to do the job, and step back. Don't hang over their shoulders. "Oh, you are doing it that way? Huh. I wouldn't." They may not do it the way you would, but they will do it.

5. Reward the Commander in a Tangible Way

A servant working in the Royal household of Prince Charles retired and, as is often the case, wrote a book about all the secrets he witnessed behind the palace walls.

One of the stories appeared in the Canadian press because it involved Prince Charles and Pierre Trudeau, a former Canadian prime minister.

The story goes that when this servant retired, his employer, Prince Charles, came to him and essentially said, "You good and faithful servant, for the long service to myself and my family, I want to give you a gift, and here it is," handing the servant a signed photo of himself, "Love, Charles."

This was something that apparently was not often given, and the servant treasured it, hanging it above his fireplace. But Charles also said to him, "I hope you don't do with this what Pierre Trudeau did with the photo I gave him."

Then he proceeded to tell his servant how when he was in Trudeau's home in Montreal for a meal and gave Trudeau a photo in like manner, how Trudeau thanked him, arose, and then went to a large bureau, opened the drawer, and threw it in. And Charles said, "And as that drawer was open, I could see every other member of my family in there, face up!"

6. Be Precise and Be On Time

If you are going to a meeting with a Commander, be on time. They will not be impressed when you shuffle in late. Time means something different to Commanders than the rest of us.

7. Discuss and Debate Outcomes

If you want to be viewed as a bore, talk process. If you want to be seen as their equal, talk big picture and bottom line. That is what is important to them.

8. To Correct, Highlight the Gap between Desired and Actual Behavior

Finally, to correct them, highlight the gap that exists between the desired and the actual. Ask for their cooperation in narrowing or closing that gap, but don't be too specific in telling them how to do so. Draw on their creative energies and need for closure and achievement, and you will generally be satisfied with the result.

If you internalize these strategies in your interactions with others, you will have greater success in your relationships. You will be a more effective negotiator, and you will experience fewer interpersonal conflicts.

The Personal Professional Dichotomy

The greater the gap between where one scores personally and where one scores professionally, the more role-stress one experiences. Statistically speaking, approximately 70% of respondents will score in the same temperament both socially and professionally, representing average role-stress. Approximately 20% of respondents will score in adjacent temperaments, indicating moderate role-stress. And approximately 10% of respondents see a gap of one or more temperaments between their personal temperament and their professional temperament. In order to determine where you fall professionally and where you fall socially, please complete the bottom line on the score sheet below.

SOCIAL PROFESSIONAL DICHOTOMY

CBSI Score Sheet

1	Sum of questions 1 through 25	**a**					
2	Sum of questions 51 through 75	**b**		**E = (a + b)**			
3	Sum of questions 26 through 50	**c**					
4	Sum of questions 76 through 100	**d**		**A = (c + d)**			
5	Ep = (Ax2)		Ap = (Cx2)		Es = (Bx2)		As = (Dx2)

INSTRUCTIONS:

Take the number you entered in the Box marked with a lowercase A on the score sheet on page 98 in this book, double that number and enter it into the box labeled Ep on line 5 above.

Next take the number you entered in the Box marked with a lowercase B on the score sheet on page 98. Double it and enter it into Box Ap.

Then take the number you had entered into the Box marked with a lowercase C, double it, and enter it into the box labeled Es.

Finally, take the number you entered into the Box marked with a lowercase D, double it, and enter it into box As.

PLOTTING YOUR PROFESSIONAL TEMPERAMENT:

Using the Behavioral Styles Matrix on page 170 or Appendix C on page 200, locate the number you entered in Box Ep above. Beginning at the red dot in the lower left-hand corner of the Matrix, move up a distance equal to that number, and make a mark.

Then, taking a ruler or hard edge, draw a horizontal line across the page through that mark.

Next, using the value you entered into Box Ap, and again starting from the dot in the lower left-hand corner, move across the Matrix to that value, and make a mark. Again, taking your ruler, draw a vertical line up the page through that mark.

The intersection of the two lines that you have just drawn marks your Professional Behavioral Style and Temperament.

PLOTTING YOUR SOCIAL TEMPERAMENT:

Using the Behavioral Styles Matrix on page 170 or Appendix C on page 200, locate the number you entered in Box Es on page 98. Beginning at the red dot in the lower left-hand corner of the Matrix, move up a distance equal to that number, and make a mark.

Then, taking a ruler or hard edge, draw a horizontal line across the page through that mark.

Next, using the value you entered into Box As, and again starting from the dot in the lower left-hand corner, move across the Matrix to that value, and make a mark. Again, taking your ruler, draw a vertical line up the page through that mark.

The intersection of the two lines that you have just drawn marks your Social Behavioral Style and Temperament.

BEHAVIORAL STYLES MATRIX®

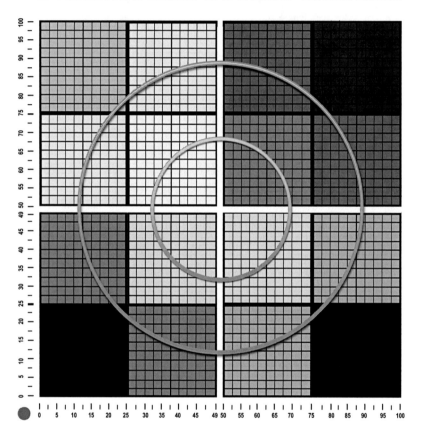

DOMINANT BEHAVIORAL STYLE:

PROFESSIONAL SUB-STYLE:

INTERPRETATION:

The question often asked is, "Where should the professional and personal points be in relationship to one another?" There's no real answer to that question. The one thing I can tell you is that statistically, the majority of people (a full 67%) will show graphically a professional (P) above and to the right of social (S).

This simply reflects the fact that most people are more emotionally responsive in their non-work (perhaps intimate relationships) than they are with those with whom they work.

Secondly, most people are more assertive in their non-work relationships than they are in their work relationships. Most people are more assertive with their spouse than their boss. Remember, I said "most people," not all people. There are many reasons why your score may not be normal in a sense.

We all play roles. The physician plays a role, the lawyer plays a role, and the administrative professional plays a role. There are certain expectations that are attached to every occupational situation. Take, for example, a police officer. To be successful in that role, the expectation is that the police officer can perform an act in an authoritarian, assertive manner. The police officer is charged with enforcing the law, not interpreting the law, and certainly not constructing the law. On the surface, it would appear that individuals coming from the Commander quadrant would be naturally more suited to this position in society than the other three. And that may very well be the case.

The reality, however, is that many police officers, perhaps even the majority, do not fall into the Commander quadrant, but the successful ones have learned to play that role well when it is appropriate to do so.

Below is an actual behavioral profile for Jeff W., a police officer who recently attended one of my management seminars. As you can see, professionally he falls clearly in the Commander quadrant, but socially he scores in the Supporter quadrant.

Compare Jeff's profile with the behavioral profile for another police officer, Janet T., who likewise is found in the Commander quadrant professionally but who is also found in the Commander quadrant socially.

While both these officers might be equally as effective in the performance of their duties, I would suggest that Jeff is more likely to experience greater workplace stress.

Every time we have to leave our comfort zone, changing who we truly are to accommodate the demands of our jobs, we place ourselves under a certain amount of stress.

Janet does not experience this stress, as with her, what you see is what you get. She does not have to play a role. She is the same socially as she is professionally.

The same could be said of administrative professionals. I think one of the reasons why "secretary" was so often spoken of pejoratively in the early days of the women's movement stemmed from the fact that many of the leaders of the women's movement could see that there were scores of intelligent, decisive women capable of managing their male bosses, forced to play a subservient role in order to be accepted to fit in the organizational environment that she found herself in.

We play roles all the time - the role of mother, father; son or daughter; husband, wife, or lover.

One of the significant features of the social/professional dichotomy is the actual distance or gap that exists between where you fall professionally and where you score socially.

The greater the gap between where one scores socially and where one scores professionally, the more role-stress one experiences. Statistically speaking, approximately 70% of respondents will score in the same temperament both socially and professionally, representing average role-stress. Approximately 20% of respondents will score in adjacent temperaments, indicating moderate role-stress. And approximately 10% of respondents see a gap of one or more temperaments between their social temperament and their professional temperament.

Jeff W. Police Officer

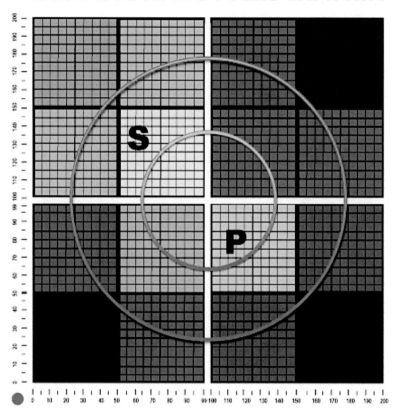

Janet T. Police Officer

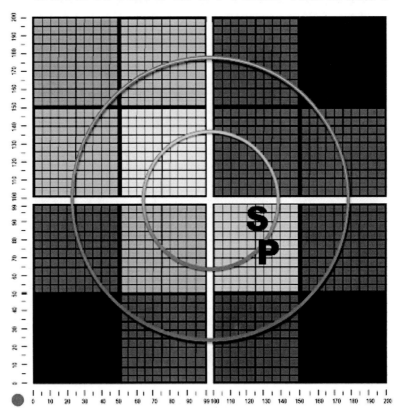

In the next chapter, we will examine how an understanding of the Behavioral Styles Model can assist you in improving work relationships with others.

The Boss
Administrative Professional Team:

Behavioral Flexibility

In this chapter, we will apply what we have learned about ourselves and the Behavioral Styles Model to create more productive boss/assistant team, however the strategies outlined here can be employed to improve relationships with co-workers, subordinates and others in your personal life. The recommendations contained in this chapter do not require that you become a human chameleon, they just ask you to temporarily take on some of the characteristics of the individual you are hoping to interact with more effectively.

The detailed recommendations contained in this chapter are provided to help you improve your communication and interpersonal relationship with the target (boss, subordinate, spouse, etc.) by applying the principles inherent in the Behavioral Styles Model. The practices and techniques suggested here are specific to your individual behavioral style and require you to understand and emulate, albeit temporarily, the style of the individual you wish to influence. By so doing, you will put that person at greater ease and make it easier for them to work with you.

The object is not to deny or lose who you are, because to do so would be to sacrifice the benefits that come, when two divergent styles work together. By removing roadblocks to effective communication, you will, however, increase cooperation and decrease misunderstanding.

It is not necessary for you to read this entire chapter; rather, simply find the combination that best fits and describes you and your boss from the chart below.

YOUR STYLE	BOSS	PAGE
SUPPORTER	SUPPORTER	178
SUPPORTER	DREAMER	179
SUPPORTER	THINKER	180
SUPPORTER	COMMANDER	181
DREAMER	SUPPORTER	182
DREAMER	DREAMER	183
DREAMER	THINKER	184
DREAMER	COMMANDER	185
THINKER	SUPPORTER	186
THINKER	DREAMER	187
THINKER	THINKER	188
THINKER	COMMANDER	189
COMMANDER	SUPPORTER	190
COMMANDER	DREAMER	191
COMMANDER	THINKER	192
COMMANDER	COMMANDER	193

 **SUPPORTER CONNECTING WITH SUPPORTER BOSS**

While counterintuitive, when two individuals with the same behavioral style work together there can be problems. They lack important differences that can actually contribute to collaboration. As a general rule in interacting with another person with the same style as your own, it can be useful to temporarily take on the characteristics of one of the other three behavioral styles. Relationships are paramount to the Supporter; their top priority is to get along. It is essential therefore in your interactions with your fellow Supporters that you show that you care for them by always framing your communication in a warm and sympathetic manner.

1. While it is not you natural approach, force yourself to ask your boss specific questions.

2. Show a sincere personal interest in them, but don't over do it.

3. When you disagree with your Supporter boss, avoid discussing your feelings; rather take a page from the Thinker's book and discuss facts.

4. Try to increase your pace from the slower more relaxed one you normally display.

5. Be more task-oriented, be on time and get right down to business paying more attention to deadlines and details than you would normally do.

6. Take time to say "thank you," your Supporter boss thrives on appreciation.

 **SUPPORTER CONNECTING WITH DREAMER BOSS**

As a Supporter you have a good deal in common with the Dreamer. You both share one of the two behavioral parameters - expressiveness. You both care about others. The Dreamer appreciates your warmth and friendliness and the fact that you too care about the impact of decisions on other staff members. The challenge in this relationship arises from the fact that, unlike yourself, the Dreamer is fast-paced, extroverted and more assertive.

1. Support your Dreamer boss's future-oriented approach. Goal attainment and what <u>could be</u> is important to them; pay careful attention to these things.

2. Tell them what you think, but try not to engage your Dreamer boss in argument as their backup or stress-style is defensiveness.

3. Take time to build personal rapport with your boss.

4. Try to demonstrate higher levels of energy - pick up the pace. By moving, speaking and deciding more rapidly you will better sync with their style.

5. Follow-up important decisions with something in writing - but keep it short.

6. Remember that the Dreamer is a person of vision - many ideas but always the means of accomplishing them. Move them toward practical ways of moving their ideas to fruition.

7. Remember too that Dreamers are not detail-oriented; they can become easily bored. Therefore, focus on the big picture and the bottom line and handle as many of the details as you can yourself.

8. Recognizing that most Dreamers tend to procrastinate; help them stay on track

 **SUPPORTER CONNECTING WITH THINKER BOSS**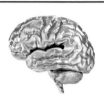

As a Supporter, you have a good deal in common with the Thinker. You both share one of the two behavioral parameters - non-assertiveness. The Dreamer will be comfortable and in sync with your thoughtful, slow-paced, non-confrontational approach. The challenge you have arises from the fact that, unlike yourself, the Thinker's priority is task, not people, as it is for you. A successful relationship with a Thinker is largely dependent on your ability to thoughtfully prepare for your interactions with them.

1. Support your boss's thoughtful, organized approach, but help them to substitute excellence for perfection.

2. Be on topic and on time, and try to be more task-oriented.

3. Play down feelings, rather, talk about what you think. Limit gestures, facial expression, eye contact, etc., and don't touch!

4. When seeking to convince them, present facts, not your feelings or other people's opinions. Provide several alternatives and the advantages and disadvantages of each.

5. Be well prepared in dealing with them - do your homework. Try to anticipate their questions and concerns. Your Thinker boss is likely to ask many questions in their search for a logical solution. Provide detail

6. Follow proper protocols and procedures, and emphasize deadlines so they can build those time frames into their procedures.

7. If dealing with an important issue, follow up with something in writing.

 **SUPPORTER CONNECTING WITH COMMANDER BOSS**

Building a workable relationship with a Commander can be a challenge for you as a Supporter insofar as you have very little in common with them. You are a non-assertive (perhaps even introverted) individual who is emotionally responsive and concerned with the impact your actions have on the feelings of others. The Commander, on the other hand, is highly assertive, extroverted, and task-oriented. Your success in your interactions with them is therefore dependent on your ability to get in touch with their non-expressive outlook and behavior.

1. Give recognition to your Commander boss's goals and objectives, but help them look past their nature competitive spirit and focus on the common goal.

2. Summon the courage to tell them what you think, and when differences arise - argue the facts, not your personal feelings.

3. Provide actions and alternatives for decision-making. Commanders like to take shortcuts; show them the quickest path to their destination. Focus on results and be pragmatic, realistic, and practical.

4. Be precise, on time, and get right down to business, emphasizing the major points.

5. Understate feelings. You will be more in sync with your Commander boss by becoming less emotionally revealing. Limit facial expression, broad gestures, and don't touch! Talk about what you think - not how you feel.

6. When seeking to influence your Commander boss, don't push too hard; provide a brief analysis of each option and describe what the relative probabilities of success are by adherence to each alternative approach.

**DREAMER
CONNECTING
WITH SUPPORTER
BOSS**

As a Dreamer, you have a good deal in common with the Supporter. You both share one of the two behavioral parameters - expressiveness. While you both care about, and like to work with others, relationships are even more important to the Supporter. Their top priority is to get along, The Supporter appreciates your warmth and friendliness and the fact that you also care about the impact of decisions on the needs and feelings of other people. The conflict arises from the fact that, unlike yourself, the Supporter is non-assertive and slow-paced, possibly introverted and certainly less assertive than you are.

1. Hard as it is for you, listen more and speak less, don't interrupt them and don't finish their sentences. Let them know that you are listening by the generous use of acknowledgements and paraphrases.

2. Try to show a sincere personal interest in them.

3. When you disagree with your Supporter boss discuss feelings as well as facts.

4. Slow your pace to match their natural slow pace. Speak slower and try not to rush them.

5. Don't come on too strong, speak softly and avoid broad gestures and intense eye contact.

6. Take time to say, "thank you," your Supporter boss thrives on appreciation.

7. Use more tentative, provisional phrasing as opposed to direct or doctrinaire language.

DREAMER CONNECTING WITH DREAMER BOSS

While counterintuitive, when two individuals with the same behavioral style work together, there can be problems. Their similarity of style can actually contribute to a lack of collaboration. As a general rule in interacting with another person with the same style as your own, it can be useful to temporarily take on the characteristics of one of the other styles. For example, when two fun-loving, lively, entertaining Dreamers work together, it might prove beneficial if one were to act more seriously to affect a better outcome. The following approaches may prove beneficial in improving your relationships with other Dreamers:

1. Support your Dreamer boss's future-oriented approach. Goal attainment and what <u>could be</u> is important to them; pay careful attention to these things.

2. Tell them what you think, but avoid power struggles. Try not to engage your Dreamer boss in argument recognizing their backup or stress-style is defensiveness.

3. Although it is neither your nature, nor that of your Dreamer boss, follow up important decisions with something in writing - but keep it short.

4. Remember that, like you, your Dreamer boss is a person of vision, they have many ideas but not always the way of accomplishing them. Move them toward practical ways of getting their ideas to fruition.

5. Remember too that since neither you nor your Dreamer boss are detail-oriented, it can help to take a page from the Thinker's book and focus on specifics.

6. As you are probably aware, Dreamers tend to procrastinate; help them stay on track.

 **DREAMER CONNECTING WITH THINKER BOSS**

Building a workable relationship with the Thinker can be a challenge for you as a Dreamer insofar as you have very little in common with them. You are an assertive and perhaps even extroverted individual. They, on the other hand, are non-assertive, emotionally non-expressive and not overly concerned with the impact their actions have on the feelings of others. Your success in interacting with them is therefore dependent on your ability to get in touch with their non-expressive outlook and non-directive behaviors.

1. Support their thoughtful organized approach, but help them to substitute excellence for perfection.

2. Listen more and listen better. Your Thinker boss expresses his or her thoughts and ideas indirectly. Invite them to speak and don't interrupt them or finish their sentences.

3. Play down feelings; rather, talk about what you think, but don't come on too strong. Limit gestures, facial expression, direct eye contact, etc., and don't touch!

4. When seeking to convince them, present facts rather than your personal feelings or the opinion of others. Provide alternatives, highlighting the advantages and disadvantages of each.

5. Be well prepared in dealing with them - do your homework. Try to anticipate their questions and concerns. Your Thinkers boss is likely to ask many questions in their search for a logical solution. Although it may not seem natural for you, focus on details and with important matters follow up in writing.

DREAMER CONNECTING WITH COMMANDER BOSS

As a Dreamer, you have a good deal in common with the Commander. You both share one of the two behavioral parameters - assertiveness. The Commander is comfortable and in sync with your direct, fast-paced, energetic approach. The challenges you will have arise from the fact that, unlike yourself, the Commander's priority is task, not people. Success in your interactions with them is dependent on your ability to get in touch with their non-expressive outlook and behavior.

1. Give recognition to your Commander boss's goals and objectives, but help them look past their natural competitive spirit and focus on the common goal.

2. When differences arise - argue the facts, not your personal feelings.

3. Provide actions and alternatives for decision-making.

4. Be precise, on time, and resist your tendency to socialize.

5. Understate feelings. You will be more in sync with your Commander boss by becoming less emotionally revealing. Limit facial expression, broad gestures, and don't touch!

6. Talk about what you think - not how you feel.

7. When seeking to influence your Commander boss, don't push too hard, provide a brief analysis of each option and describe what you see to be the relative probabilities of success by adherence to each alternative. Don't inundate them with data.

8. Discuss and debate outcomes - not procedures. Help them focus on the results of their actions and be realistic and pragmatic. Be cognizant of and avoid, power struggles.

THINKER CONNECTING WITH THINKER BOSS

As a Thinker, you have a great deal in common with the Supporter. You share one of the two basic dimensions of style - assertiveness, or more accurately in this case, non-assertiveness. You are both introverted and slower-paced individuals. The Supporter appreciates the fact that you are not pushy or threatening and have similar pacing. The conflict stems from the fact that, unlike you, the Supporter is people-oriented and emotionally responsive. Relationships are paramount to the Supporter; their top priority is to get along.

1. Take time to build personal rapport with your Supporter boss. Share something about yourself or your personal life. Try to be a little less formal than you normally are.

2. Take a sincere personal interest in them and focus on feelings not just facts.

3. When you disagree with your Supporter boss, discuss feelings as well as facts.

4. Actively listen to them, asking them how they feel about things.

5. Seek opportunities to compliment their people skills.

6. Take time to say "thank you," your Supporter boss thrives on appreciation.

THINKER
CONNECTING
WITH DREAMER
BOSS

Building a workable relationship with a Dreamer can be challenging for you as a Thinker, inasmuch as you have very little in common with them. You are a non-assertive (and often an introverted) individual, emotionally non-expressive, concerned with solving problems and getting the task accomplished, while the Dreamer is highly assertive, extroverted, and people-oriented. The following approaches, however, have been proven effective:

1. Support your Dreamer boss's future-oriented approach. Goal attainment and what <u>could be</u> is important to them; pay careful attention to these things.

2. Take time to build personal rapport with your boss. Share something about yourself or your personal life and try to be a little less formal.

3. When you disagree with your Dreamer boss, discuss feelings as well as facts. Try not to engage the Dreamer in argument as their backup or stress-style is defensiveness.

3. Although it is not their natural tendency nor is it yours, follow-up important decisions with something in writing - but keep it short.

4. Remember that your Dreamer boss is a person of vision - many ideas but not always the means of accomplishing them. Move them toward practical ways of bringing their ideas to fruition.

5. Remember, too, that unlike you, the Dreamer is not detail-oriented. You can help them a great deal by moving the conversation to the specifics.

DREAMER CONNECTING WITH THINKER BOSS

While counterintuitive, when two individuals with the same behavioral style work together, there can be problems. They lack important differences that can actually contribute to collaboration. As a general rule, in interacting with another person with the same style as your own, it can be useful to briefly take on the characteristics of one of the other styles. For example, when two task-oriented, slow-paced Thinkers work together, it might prove beneficial to temporarily take on the style of the Commander, assume some risk, and push for action. Your successful relationship with the Thinker is largely dependent on your ability to thoughtfully prepare for your interactions with them.

1. Support your boss's thoughtful organized approach, but challenge the need for so much detail; help them substitute excellence for perfection.

2. Listen more and listen better. Your Thinker boss expresses his or her thoughts and ideas indirectly. Invite them to speak, and don't interrupt them or finish their sentences.

3. When seeking to convince them, present facts, but also shine the spotlight on the human impact of their decisions.

4. Be well prepared in dealing with them - do your homework. Try to anticipate their questions and concerns. As you know, Thinkers are likely to ask many questions in their search for a logical conclusion. Follow up important decisions with something in writing.

5. Follow proper protocols and procedures, and emphasize deadlines so they can build those time frames into their procedures.

THINKER CONNECTING WITH COMMANDER BOSS

As a Thinker, you have a good deal in common with the Commander. You are both task-oriented and non-expressive. Commanders are comfortable and in sync with your thoughtful, problem-solving approach. The challenge in this relationship arises from the fact that, unlike yourself, the Commander is more assertive than you. Your success in your interactions with the Commander is dependent on your ability to get in touch with their non-expressive outlook and behavior.

1. Give recognition to your Commander boss's goals and objectives, and help them look past their natural competitive spirit and focus on the common goal.

2. Summon the courage to tell them what you think, voice your concerns and try to be more direct and less tentative. Ask fewer questions.

3. Provide actions and alternatives for decision-making. Commanders like to take shortcuts; show them the quickest path to their destination, and help them focus on the human impact of their decisions.

4. Pick up the pace, speak more quickly, and try to make and implement decisions more rapidly.

5. Try talking about what you feel - not just what you think.

6. When seeking to influence your Commander boss, don't push too hard, rather, provide a brief analysis of each option and describe what you see to be the relative probabilities of success by adherence to each. Don't inundate them with information.

COMMANDER
CONNECTING
WITH SUPPORTER
BOSS

Building a workable relationship with a Supporter can be challenging for you as a Commander, inasmuch as you have very little in common with them. You are an assertive (and often an extroverted) individual, emotionally non-expressive, concerned with achievement, goal accomplishment, and success, while the Supporter is non-assertive, introverted, and people-oriented. The following approaches, however, have been proven effective:

1. Take time to build personal rapport with your Supporter boss. Share something about yourself or your personal life. Try to be a little less formal and try also not to come across as aloof.

2. Take a sincere personal interest in them and focus on feelings not just facts, projects or priorities.

3. When you disagree with your Supporter boss, discuss feelings and the human impact of your mutual efforts.

4. You are a strong, self-directed individual, but try not to come on too strong. Speak more softly; avoid intense eye contact, and phrase things more tentatively and in a less inflexible or opinionated way.

5. Speak less and take time to actively listen to them. Ask them how they feel about things. Don't interrupt them or finish their sentences.

COMMANDER CONNECTING WITH DREAMER BOSS

As a Commander, you have a good deal in common with the Dreamer. You both share one of the two behavioral parameters - assertiveness. Dreamers are comfortable and in sync with your fast-paced, assertive approach. The challenge you have arises from the fact that, unlike yourself, the Dreamer is more emotionally responsive and expressive than you are.

1. Support your Dreamer boss's spontaneous, future-oriented approach, but keep them grounded by following up important matters with something in writing - but keep it short.

2. Tell them what you think, but try not to engage your boss in argument as their backup or stress-style is defensiveness.

3. Take time to build personal rapport with your Dreamer boss. Share something about yourself or your personal life. Try to be a little less formal.

4. Take a sincere personal interest in them and focus on feelings, not just facts or the job at hand.

5. Remember that the Dreamer boss is a person of vision - many ideas but not always the means of accomplishing them. Move them towards practical ways of bringing their ideas to fruition.

6. Remember also that Dreamers are not detail-oriented. They become easily bored. Talk about the big picture and the bottom line, and handle as many of the details as you can yourself.

8. Recognize that most Dreamers tend to procrastinate; help them stay on track with friendly reminders.

COMMANDER CONNECTING WITH THINKER BOSS

You have a great deal in common with the Thinker. As a Commander, your priorities are the same. You both are task-oriented and concerned with getting things done. The conflict comes from the fact that you are much more assertive than the Thinker. Your successful relationship with the Thinker is largely dependent on your ability to thoughtfully prepare for your interactions with them.

1. Support your boss's thoughtful, organized approach, but challenge the need for so much detail; help them to substitute excellence for perfection.

2. Listen more and listen better. Your Thinker boss expresses his or her thoughts and ideas indirectly. Invite them to speak and don't interrupt them or finish their sentences.

3. You are a strong, self-directed individual, but try not to come on too strong. Speak more softly; avoid intense eye contact and phrase things more tentatively and in a less inflexible or opinionated way.

4. When seeking to convince them, present facts, but also shine the spotlight on the human impact of their decisions. Provide several alternatives and the advantages and disadvantages of each.

5. Be well prepared in dealing with your boss - do your homework. Try to anticipate their questions and concerns. Thinkers are likely to ask many questions in their search for a logical solution. Possibly follow up in writing.

COMMANDER CONNECTING WITH COMMANDER BOSS

While counterintuitive, when two individuals with the same behavioral style work together, there can be problems. They lack important differences that can actually contribute to collaboration. As a general rule, in interacting with another person with the same style as your own, it can be useful to temporarily take on the characteristics of one of the other styles. For example, as you are both very decisive, it might improve the quality of your decisions if you were to take a page from the Thinker's playbook and push for further information and data before making the decision.

1. Give recognition to your Commander boss's goals and objectives, and help them look past their natural competitive spirit and focus on the common goal.

2. Provide actions and alternatives for decision-making. As you know, Commanders like to take shortcuts; show them the quickest path to their destination. Focus on results and be pragmatic, realistic, and practical.

3. Shine the spotlight on the human impact of your decisions, and how it can actually improve the quality of those decisions. In this regard, try to talk about how you feel, not just what you think.

5. Be precise, on time, and get right down to business, emphasizing the major issues and skipping the details.

7. When seeking to influence your Commander boss, don't push too hard; rather, provide a brief analysis of each option and describe what you see to be the relative probabilities of success by their adherence to each alternative. Remember that, like you, the Commander only wants the information necessary to act. Don't inundate them with details.

Chapter 11

Conclusion

The role of the administrative professional has changed dramatically over the past two decades, and it continues to evolve following a trajectory put in place by organizational re-adjustments and societal changes.

The responsibilities the administrative professional has to shoulder are becoming more complex as the workplace continues to transform, yet today's administrative professional is less of a specialist than her secretarial predecessors. Today's administrative professional is a generalist who must not only cope in an ever-changing environment but who must deal effectively with different and sometimes difficult people within the organization and at the interface or boundary with the external world.

Having said this, it follows that there is no more important skill the administrative professional must possess than highly developed people skills, specifically what we call "emotional intelligence."

In this book, we have examined in some detail the four components of emotional intelligence.

We have provided you one of the most useful self-awareness constructs available today – the Behavioral Styles Model. We have discussed how an understanding of this model can help you identify who the key actors in our life are in a behavioral sense. And, most importantly, we have provided specific recommendations for improving your communications with them.

The Behavioral Styles Model does not ask you to try to change anyone - it only asks that you temporarily change yourself.

As you practice the precepts and the principles that form the basis of the Behavioral Styles Model, your social awareness will expand, and you will find it becomes much easier to identify others' styles, and you will become more adept in managing yourself and your emotions as you more effectively manage your relationships.

The greatest achievement we can have in life is to help others succeed and grow and learn and to know ourselves.

As the great philosopher Soren Kierkegaard[14] once said, the purpose of life is to be that self which one truly is.

I hope that this book has helped you know that self a little better.

References

1. United States Census 2006, "Married Couple Family Groups, by Presence of Own Children/1 In Specific Age Groups, and Age, Earnings, Education, and Race and Hispanic Origin of Both Spouses: 2006."

2. Chiao, Vani A. Mathur, Tokiko Harada and Trixie Lipke" of Northwestern's Department of Psychology. Neural Basis of Extraordinary Empathy and Altruistic Motivation," was published in March in the journal NeuroImage.

3. Bell, Daniel. "The Coming of Post-Industrial Society." New York: Harper Colophon Books, 1974

4. Psychologists John (Jack) Mayer, Ph.D., of the University of New Hampshire and Peter Salovey, Ph.D. of Yale University published two academic papers on emotional intelligence in 1990. Salovey and Mayer defined emotional intelligence as the: "Ability to monitor one's own and other's feelings and emotions, to discriminate among them and to use this information to guide one's thinking and actions." (1990).

5. Gardner, Howard (1983; 1993) Frames of Mind: The theory of multiple intelligences, New York: Basic Books. A major addition to the literature of cognitive psychology being the first full-length explication of multiple intelligences.

6. Salovey, P., Mayer, J.D., & Caruso, D.R. (2008). Emotional Intelligence: New ability or eclectic traits, American Psychologist, 63, 6, 503-517.Mayer, John D.

7. Mayer, J. D., Salovey, P., Hsee, C., & (1993). Emotional intelligence and the self- regulation of affect. In D.M. Wegner & J.W. Pennebaker (Eds.) Handbook of mental control (Pp. 258-277). Englewood Cliffs, NJ: Prentice-Hall.

8. Caruso, D.R., Mayer, J.D., & Salovey, P. (2002). Relation of an ability measure of emotional intelligence to personality. Journal of Personality Assessment, 79, 306-320

9. Goleman, D. (1995). Emotional intelligence. New York: Bantam Book

10. Spady, W. (1998). Paradigm lost: Reclaiming America's educational future. Arlington, VA: American Association of School Administrators.

11. Arnold, K.D. (1995). Lives of promise: What becomes of high school valedictorians. San Francisco: Jossey-Bass.

12. Jung, C.G. (1916). Collected Papers on Analytical Psychology. Bailliere, Tindall and Cox.

13. Blake, R.; Mouton, J. (1964). The Managerial Grid: The Key to Leadership Excellence. Houston: Gulf Publishing Co.

14. A famous series of studies on leadership were done in Ohio State University, starting in the 1950s. They found two critical characteristics either of which could be high or low and were independent of one another. The research was base on questionnaires to leaders and subordinates. These are known as the Leader Behavior Description Questionnaire (LDBQ).

15. Kierkegaard, Søren. (2001). A Literary Review. London: Penguin Classics.

Appendix A

EMOTIONAL INTELLIGENCE ASSESSMENT

A	SELF-AWARENESS

B	SELF-MANAGEMENT

C	SOCIAL AWARENESS

D	RELATIONSHIP MANAGEMENT

```
| | | | | | | | | | | | | | | | | | | | | | | | | | | | | | | | | | | | | | | |
0               5              10              15              20
```

EQ	EMOTIONAL INTELLIGENCE

```
| | | | | | | | | | | | | | | | | | | | | | | | | | | | | | | | | | | | | | | |
0        10       20       30       40       50       60       70       80
```

A	Sum of Questions:	**1 - 10**	
B	Sum of Questions:	**11 - 20**	
C	Sum of Questions:	**21 - 30**	
D	Sum of Questions:	**31 - 40**	
EQ	TOTAL:	**1 - 40**	

Appendix B

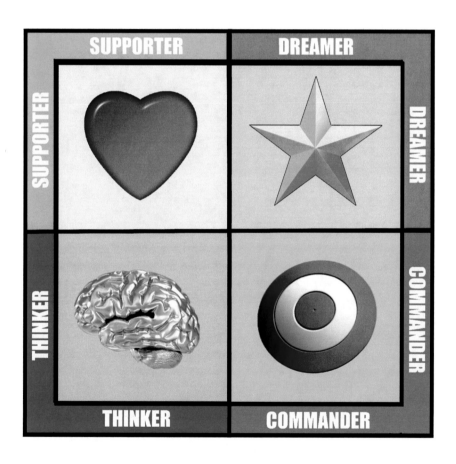

Appendix C

Comprehensive Behavioral Styles Inventory™
360° Emotional Intelligence Assessment

BEHAVIORAL STYLES MATRIX®

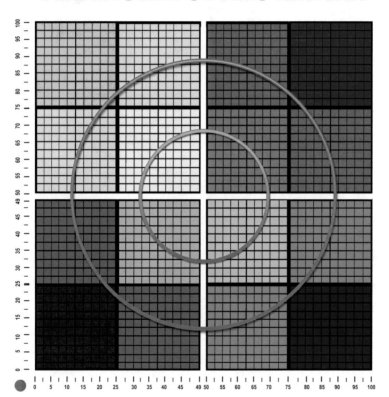

DOMINANT BEHAVIORAL STYLE: [ ]

PROFESSIONAL SUB-STYLE: [ ]

Appendix D

The Sixteen Temperaments

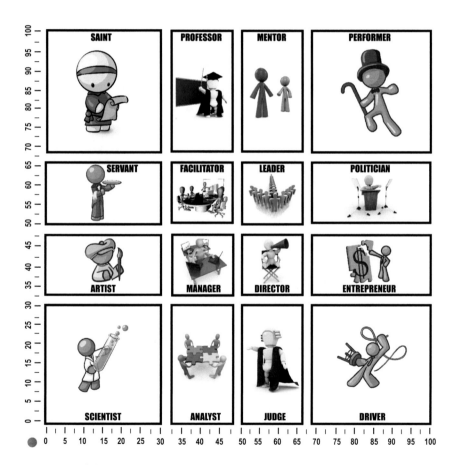

Index

Comprehensive Behavioral Styles Inventory™
360° Emotional Intelligence Assessment

cbsp™

CBSI Booklets

Additional copies of this **Comprehensive Behavioral Styles Inventory** may be purchased at the workshop
or on-line at www.mycbsp.com. The Comprehensive Behavioral Styles Profile (CBSI) is used by many organizations,
large and small, because it provides a framework for understanding and reconciling individual differences as well as

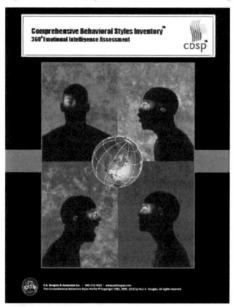

providing a dynamic model for individual and
organizational development. The CBSI can
support many organizational functions
including conflict resolution, training, team-
building and the development of leadership
skills.

ORDER NOW AT: www.mycbsp.com
or by calling: 1-800-222-4062

CBSI - 1 to 20 copies	$19.95 ea.
CBSI - 21 to 40 copies	$14.95 ea.
CBSI - 41 to 99 copies	$12.95 ea.
CBSI - 100 plus copies	$10.95 ea.

About Paul A. Douglas

Paul Douglas is an internationally acclaimed author, speaker and consultant to scores of major corporations, universities and governments. His unique and effective approach to leadership training emphasizing the "people skills" of good management as well as strategic excellence has benefited thousands of managers and administrative professionals. He is a Certified Management Consultant (CMC) and holds a Bachelor of Commerce (B.Com.) and Master of Business Administration (MBA) degree from the University of Alberta where he taught in the Faculty of Business. He also has a doctorate (Ph.D.) in business administration and organizational psychology.